# TRANSFORMATION:
## A New Creation in Christ
### The Journey from Easter to Pentecost

VELMA RUCH
Editor

Herald Publishing House, Independence 64051


Printed in the United States of America

11 10 09 08 07 06 5 4 3 2 1

Library of Congress Cataloging-in-Publication Data

Transformation : a new creation in Christ : the journey from Easter to Pentecost / [edited] by Velma Ruch.
p. cm.
Includes index.
ISBN-13: 978-0-8309-1231-5
ISBN-10: 0-8309-1231-2
1. Resurrection--Meditations. 2. Ascension--Meditations. 3. Pentecost--Meditations. I. Ruch, Velma.
BT482.T73 2006
242'.3--dc22
2006005151



Transformation: A New Creation in Christ
The Journey from Easter to Pentecost

ISBN-10: 0-8309-1231-2
ISBN-13: 978-0-8309-1231-5

# Acknowledgments

All of us, regardless of denomination, are blessed with a treasure of thoughtful and creative writing contributed by Christian scholars dedicated to spiritual formation.and a deeper understanding of Christian discipleship. In assembling the materials for these meditations I searched once again through books and periodicals that had become precious to me to sort out and share with the readers of this volume the heart of some of these writings. The authors whose works are cited here are too many to mention, but they are listed in the body of the work as well as in the bibliography. As I have sorted through my own writings to find material that might be worth saying once again I was struck by the many, both living and dead, who have deeply influenced me and whose words speak through my own. The Scriptures, which form the core of this material, are supreme among these. I have used the three books sacred to the Community of Christ: The Bible, The Book of Mormon, and The Doctrine and Covenants. It is my prayer that you will find renewed appreciation for these volumes as you open yourself to their spiritual wisdom once again.

I wish to express special appreciation to Scott Murphy, president of the Lamoni Heartland Mission Center for appointing and supporting a spiritual formation committee; for Dick Young who chaired that committee, and for the individual members whose thoughts spurred me to these writings. Special appreciation goes to Rich Brown and his associates at Herald House who accepted this work for publication and asked me to write two additional volumes. When under the pressure of church finance, publication was put on hold, many offered to pay for publication costs if Graceland University's Media Center could assist in preparing the material for publication. That came to pass under the leadership of Dennis Piepergerdes and his dedicated staff. Special appreciation goes to Steve Edwards who designed the cover and planned the layout. Church leaders and Herald House staff are overseeing the publication and distribution of the material.. My deep gratitude goes to them all and to the many unnamed who have given their time and effort to this project.

# CONTENTS

# TRANSFORMATION: A NEW CREATION IN CHRIST
## THE JOURNEY FROM EASTER TO PENTECOST

## INTRODUCTION

**In an article in the *Herald* ("My Peace I Give to You," January 2005) David Schaal captured the underlying purpose of these meditations. He wrote,**

> It is critical for the church and its members to engage our world with great energy and vigor, while at the same time carving out priority time for reflection and prayer. No relationship can be healthy if we do not invest time in it. Hence, our need to be intentional about making time for meditation and prayer in order to cultivate an inner stillness in the midst of busy living. In so doing, we become more able to sense how Christ is present in the midst of the world's need and thereby become more able to receive the peace of Christ even in the presence of great turmoil (p. 13).

Worship and mission are inextricably entwined. We need not give up one to have the other. Martin Luther, for instance, found that the busier he got the more he needed his prayer time. For him, three hours a day for prayer was barely enough. Few of us today can spare that much out of our day's responsibilities. That is where the spiritual discipline of practicing the presence becomes so important. By being "intentional" about our meditation and prayer, however long, we become focused on response to the Spirit and over time learn to bring that focus into everything we do. As Brother Lawrence found (*Practicing the Presence*) that does not happen automatically and at times can seem frustrating, but nothing else in which we engage is so rich in blessing and spiritual health.

In these meditations I am using the liturgical church year as a focus for our time for reflection and prayer, I am attempting to relate our individual journeys to the mystery of the ages, particularly as reflected through the life, death, and resurrection of Christ. If we pay attention and if we take time to learn how to translate what took place so long ago into significance for us today, we, too, may have an Emmaus experience as did the two disciples whose hearts burned within them as they walked the way with Christ.

In the first volume in this series, *We Journey with Christ: Lenten and Easter Meditations*, we were present with the shepherds and wise men as they worshiped the Holy Child and in imagination participated in the growth of this child who grew in "wisdom and stature." In walking the roads of Galilee with Jesus and the disciples, we learned something about the challenge and cost of discipleship. Reflected through the lens of scripture and the words of those who had also walked this way we saw ourselves and our own lives more clearly. It was not always easy and we, like the disciples of old, were aware of how often we had made mistakes and faltered along the way. We were lost, but we were also found. We walked with Jesus in the wilderness and were tested there. We learned what it meant to remain steadfast amidst great difficulty. From the disciples and their Master, we learned lessons of love, of forgiveness, of submission, of companionship, of miracle and mystery, and finally of great suffering at the time of the crucifixion. We discovered once again what it means to have dreams shattered and to despair. But there was hope. If Friday comes, we have learned to say, Sunday cannot be far behind. To the amazement and disbelief of all, the One who had died rose again. Sorrow was turned to joy but it was a joy that was three-parts pain. There was so much to absorb and comprehend. The disciples had been thrust into the heart of mystery and it took time to adjust to the brilliance of that light. How that adjustment took place and eventually led to the flames of Pentecost is the theme of this second volume: *Transformation: A New Creation in Christ.* A third volume, *Finding Home: Meditations for Advent, Christmas, and Epiphany* will be the last in the series.

All three books have similar objectives, the most important of which is engaging readers in intentional spiritual formation on a daily basis. The basic spiritual discipline involved is what our forebears called *lectio divina*, spiritual reading. That reading most often involves scripture but includes "other good books." As members of the Community of Christ we are told to "*seek out of the best books words of wisdom; seek learning even by study, and also by faith*" (Doctrine and Covenants 85:36a). This is all for the purpose that we "*may be prepared in all things when I shall send you again, to magnify the calling whereunto I have called you, and the mission with which I have commissioned you*" (Section 85:21e).

The readings assembled to support the scriptures cited may be used both for informational and formational purposes. Their main object, however, is to lead the worshiper into a deeper relationship with the Divine. Two forms of knowledge are involved here: rational and relational. One we know by study, the other by faith. Love is relational and God is love. The only sure foundation any of us has is a person-to-Person meeting with a love that is beyond all human love, a love that touches us at the center of our being and assures us that underneath are the ever-lasting arms. Having once experienced that Center of Being, we are called to nourish that Presence and prepare ourselves to receive. Each day has enough material for an extended period of worship or for intensive focus on a short selection of scripture or a brief reading. Any or all of the spiritual disciplines (prayer, spiritual reading, study, examen, journaling, action, etc.) can be used according to the personality or needs of the individual. Each one of us begins where we are and grow from there. May you find joy in the journey.

Velma Ruch

## THE CHURCH YEAR

Religious traditions the world over have created a latticework of windows in time – holy days and seasons –through which we peer into the mystery at the heart of all that is...The natural rhythms of the days, night and seasons become the vessels in which the sacred story of God-with-us is manifest ...Through this dramatic medium we are carried into the timelessness that surrounds historic time. Human and Divine meet and touch. The liturgical year is the medium through which the Christian community sanctifies time – makes it holy.

Liturgical time also sanctifies those who enter into it. To venture into the movement of the church calendar is to risk transformation through the divine touch. It is to be ushered into the dynamics of incarnation, death, resurrection, and enspiriting ...Each year brings a new learning, a new changing, a new grasp of the meaning encoded in the rituals, hymns, prayers, images and texts particular to each holy day ...Gradually we have the threads of our own small stories woven into the tapestry of the great stories of the faith. The layers of our lives are sewn together by the stitching of the Christian year.

Wendy M. Wright, *The Rising* (Nashville: Upper Room Books, 1994), 11

## LIVING THE DAY FROM THE HEART

How do we speak of the unspeakable – of that which is closer to us than our thoughts? Such is our dilemma when we try to communicate with one another about God's presence and ways with us. Fortunately, the overlapping words and insights of scripture and spiritual tradition help us find some common language about our experience, along with engendering hopefulness about what happens in us at this most intimate level of our being ...

Contemplation is the ever-fresh world of the spiritual heart. Non-contemplation is the ever-constricted world of the head, senses and feelings separated from that heart. The spiritual heart is the true center of our being. It is the placeless place where divine Spirit and human spirit live together. When the great historical spiritual elders of the church advocated keeping the mind in the heart, I believe they were speaking of the need to keep our thoughts, feelings, bodies, actions, wills and sense of identity connected with our spiritual heart day by day, moment by moment. Our sanity and authentic discernment, love, and delight depend on this connectedness ...

The most fundamental step I believe we can take toward opening our spiritual heart is to open our longing for God: our yearning for God's fullness in us and the world, through and beyond every desire we may have. That longing is placed deep in us as a reflection of God's wondrous, loving desire to be full in us. ...When we awaken in the morning and myriad thoughts and feelings pass through our minds, our first spiritual task is to be in touch with our desire for God right through that stream of consciousness. As this happens, we touch into our spiritual heart. There we can let whatever is passing through our minds be very simply opened, offered to God. Our consciousness expands to include God. We can consecrate ourselves then to God's immediately present, pervasive love through all that registers in our minds. Then we are saved from beginning the day on some seemingly autonomous track of worry and driven activity. We begin instead with our trust that God, manifest in Christ's living Spirit, is mysteriously with and for us right now, wanting to share the day ...

Beside the fundamental need for prayer to remember our depth and desire in God and for our open hopefulness during the day, we may be drawn to a variety of other aids for living out of the collaborative, delicate place of our spiritual heart. Any of the classical spiritual disciplines for attentiveness to help us remember our intention for God may be included here: praying with scripture; other spiritual reading, worded, imaged, and formless kinds of personal and corporate prayer; journal keeping, icons and other art forms; recollecting interior words, images and objects that we carry through the day; and anything else that can help us live in touch with our heart ...We find that we are given a kind of knowing and belonging in our spiritual heart that is too fine for our minds to comprehend, yet profoundly substantial. We are being taught in God's own language, which only the heart can apprehend and there we are slowly being transformed from the image to the likeness of God, our unique Christ-nature.

Excerpts from Tilden Edwards, "Living the Day from the Heart" from *The Weavings Reader: Living with God in the World,* John S. Mogabgab, ed. (The Upper Room, 1993), 55-61; used with permission

# DAILY WORSHIP

# EASTER OCTAVE:
# THE FIRST WEEK AFTER EASTER
## THEME: RESURRECTION APEARANCES

### THE EASTER OCTAVE

Yesterday we celebrated Easter and the glory of the Resurrection. Today we are on the way to Pentecost. In many churches Easter is celebrated for eight days – from Easter Sunday through the following Sunday. It is known as the Easter Octave. Somehow one day is not enough to sing our alleluias and express our joy of the Resurrection and then on Monday go back to work, pick up old problems, and act as if nothing happened. Easter among the disciples inaugurated a fifty-day period of significant change and growth helping prepare them for the ascension of Christ and the coming of the Holy Spirit on the day we refer to as Pentecost. As we look at their journey we can also learn a great deal about our own as we progress on this challenging road to love, joy, and peace. Let us take some time to live with a few of the disciples as they come to terms with the death and resurrection of their dearest friend.

---

# MONDAY, EASTER OCTAVE:
# TRANSFORMATION OF THE DISCIPLES

**The Beginning of a New Relationship with Christ**

[There are many incidents] in the period between Easter and Pentecost, in which we are meant to see the disciples of the Lord coming of age. In their case, they had the privilege of telescoping a lot of experience into a few days or weeks. They seem to pass from infancy to spiritual maturity in fifty days. No doubt there was good reason in their case for such an accelerated course. But experience seems to indicate that after the time of that first Pentecost, it takes the best of Christians closer to fifty years ...

What took place in the souls of the disciples during those fifty days between Easter and Pentecost is taking place in us. At some point in our spiritual growth Jesus asks us to adjust ourselves to a new relationship with himself. Since this happens without much warning, almost no one has any awareness of what is taking place when it actually happens. It comes on gradually, slowly but surely. However, we can so successfully distract ourselves from our interior life that we actually never make the adjustment and never forge the new relationship Jesus asks of us ... What needs to be done here is simply to realize that the old relationship has indeed come to an end; that God wants it to come to an end; and that he wants us to climb up to a new relationship based on a new growth, on a new maturity. On the basis of this new growth all the facets of one's life must progress. This is a great struggle. Sometimes it may seem impossible. God inspires us, if we are faithful to grace, to work it out.

Thomas Keating, *Crisis of Faith, Crisis of Love*
(New York: Continuum Publishing Co., 1995), 9-12

**Seed of Promise**

*Peace I leave with you; my peace I give to you. I do not give to you as the world gives. Do not let your hearts be troubled, and do not let them be afraid.*
(John 14:27)

**SCRIPTURE:** **John 20:19-23 Jesus Stood Among Them**
*Jesus came and stood among them and said, "Peace be with you."*
**Luke 24:36-49 The Fulfilling of Prophecy**
*Then he said to them, "These are my words that I spoke to you while I was still with you – that everything written about me in the law of Moses, the prophets, and the psalms must be fulfilled." Then he opened their minds to understand the scriptures.*

**MEDITATION: "Peace Be With You"**

When Christ died on the tree of the cross, all the hopes and dreams of the disciples were shattered. Their courageous zeal yielded to fear and listlessness. Their confidence gave way to disbelief and doubt. Locked, indeed, in their own powerlessness, the disciples were dispirited. It was as if when Jesus died they lost their soul. Where had it all gone?

*"Peace be with you."*

Jesus enters through the locked door of the disciples' hearts. He pierces their fear and seizes hold of them. In his presence the walls of their confinement tumble. This is Jesus of Nazareth! He stands before them, risen in power yet bearing his wounds. Transfixed by his risen presence, the disciples are delivered into enthralling ecstatic joy!

He had promised his beloved disciples at their last meal together that he would return. He had promised that he would bring them a peace that would heal and strengthen them beyond their most cherished dreams. Now he is before them. "*Peace be with you.*" …

The moment when the disciples were given birth has now suddenly come to fullness. Through the breath of Christ, they receive the life and power of the Spirit. The new creation has begun.

Jaqueline Syrup Bergan and S. Marie Schwan, *Freedom: A Guide to Prayer*
(St. Mary's Press, 1988), 68-69

**Share the Peace of Jesus Christ**

Share …share peace …share the peace of Jesus Christ! That's it! No new programs, no new goals, no new themes, no new logos …just being faithful. Being faithful to God, being faithful to the gospel of Jesus Christ, and being faithful to the central mission of the Restoration. …

The phrase "the peace of Jesus Christ" contains all of the promises, hopes, and blessings of the gospel as revealed by Christ and affirmed by the Holy Spirit, his promised presence with us. In all of the places in our lives where we are afraid, anxious, discouraged, guilt-ridden, or alienated, Jesus Christ speaks "peace" and opens the way to peace, not just for individuals but for the whole of creation … Through Christ, something not fully explainable, but utterly transforming, has occurred. It can best be described as the movement of God to bring reconciliation and wholeness into all dimensions of life.

We begin to experience the peace of Jesus Christ as we are being reconciled to God, to others, to ourselves, and to creation. This is the heart of the gospel as we are called to live it and to proclaim it …

So what will it take to be successful in this mission? We must start with ourselves. The call of discipleship is the call to attach our lives fully and completely to Jesus Christ. Are we experiencing the power of Jesus Christ in our heart, mind, and soul? Discipleship must be grounded in intentional spiritual formation that centers us in the presence of God, where we find inner peace. It is out of the depth and overflow of this peace that we find the capacity to cope with life and to extend ourselves in the ministry of Jesus Christ in the world.

We also must recover our passion for sharing the gospel with others in those parts of the world where the spirit of evangelism has waned. How do we do that? Again, it comes through spiritual formation. If we deepen our experience with Christ through creative prayer, scripture, study, worship, Sabbath keeping, and life in community, we will discover the love and joy of the gospel bubbling up in our souls and flowing naturally into the lives of our neighbors and friends. The key to evangelism is joyful, loving disciples who are constantly inviting others to come with them to the source of true life …

I am ready to respond to the call to share the peace of Jesus Christ. *Are you?*

Excerpts from the inaugural sermon by Stephen M. Veazey, prophet-president of the Community of Christ, June 4, 2005, in Independence, Missouri

In these scripture readings and meditations, you are invited to ground your discipleship in intentional spiritual formation. In his first appearance to the disciples after his resurrection Christ gifted them with peace and the Holy Spirit. The two are inextricably related. Remember again the words of Jesus that holy night:

> *"Then the disciples rejoiced when they saw the Lord. Jesus said to them again, "Peace be with you. As the Father has sent me so send I you." When he had said this, he breathed on them and said to them, "Receive the Holy Spirit. If you forgive the sins of any, they are forgiven them; if you retain the sins of any, they are retained."*
>
> John 20:20-23

Let the words of Jesus and the call of President Veazey sink into your hearts as you allow the presence of Christ full room to dwell in you.

**PRAYER:** Loving God, our Creator and Redeemer, we, like your disciples of old, are entering on a journey of transformation. Over and over again we have heard your still, small voice urging us to come up higher, to open ourselves more completely to the One who stands knocking at our door. Be with us in these days of meditation and prayer that we may truly prepare ourselves to open the door of our hearts and like those early disciples grow in likeness to you, we pray. Amen.

# TUESDAY, EASTER OCTAVE: THE ROAD TO EMMAUS

**Call to Scripture**

We should search the Scriptures carefully in humility and with the counsel of experienced people, learning not merely theoretically but by putting into practice what we read.

(Peter of Damaskos, twelfth century)

**SCRIPTURE:** **Luke 24:13-27 Jesus Himself Came Near**

*Now on the same day two of them were going to a village called Emmaus, about seven miles from Jerusalem, and talking with each other about all these things that had happened. While they were talking and discussing, Jesus himself came near and went with them, but their eyes were kept from recognizing him.*

**MEDITATION: Who Is the Third Who Walks Always Beside You?**

Who is the third who walks always beside you?
When I count, there are only you and I together
But when I look ahead up the white road
There is always another one walking beside you
Gliding wrapt in a brown mantle, hooded.
I do not know whether a man or a woman.
But who is that on the other side of you?
T. S. Eliot. "What the Thunder Said" in *The Waste Land* (1922)

**The Emmaus Road of Long Ago**

As the two travelers walk home mourning their loss, Jesus comes up and walks by their side, but their eyes are prevented from recognizing him. Suddenly there are no longer two but three people walking, and everything becomes different. The two friends no longer look down at the ground in front of them but into the eyes of the stranger who has joined them and asked, "What are all these things you are discussing as you walk along?" There is some astonishment, even agitation: "You must be the only person who does not know the things that have been happening!" Then there follows a long story: the story of loss, the story of puzzling news about an empty tomb. Here at least is someone to listen, someone who is willing to hear the words of disillusionment, sadness, and utter confusion. Nothing seems to make sense. But it is better to tell a stranger than to repeat the known facts to each other.

Then something happens! Something shifts. The stranger begins to speak, and his words ask for serious attention. He had listened to them: now they listened to him His words are very clear and straightforward. He speaks of things they already knew; their long past with all that had happened during the centuries before they were born, the story of Moses who led their people to freedom, and the story of the prophets who challenged their people never to let go of their dearly acquired freedom. It was an all-too-familiar story. Still it sounds as if they were hearing it for the first time ...What had seemed so confusing began to offer new horizons: what had seemed so oppressive began to feel liberating; what had seemed so extremely sad began to take on the quality of joy! As he talked to them, they gradually came to know that their little lives weren't as little as they had thought, but part of a great mystery that not only embraced many generations, but stretched itself out from eternity to eternity (39-40)

Henri J. M. Nouwen, *With Burning Hearts: A Meditation on the Eucharistic Life* (Maryknoll, New York: Orbis Books, 1994), 39-40; used with permission

**Our Emmaus Road**

How many times on our network of roads have we lurched with broken spirits because the unexpected seized the place of the expected and that with a wrenching disappointment? In such moods even if what was expected then comes to us, we cannot see it. It is unrecognizable to our pain and our splintered hopes and wishes, all of which had taken on a certain shape. What should have been familiar because it was what we longed to see and consistently prayed for, is unfamiliar to us, a stranger. Two disciples ...are walking the seven miles between Jerusalem and Emmaus. They are despondent due to Christ's death. A stranger joins them who, instead of being sympathetic, bursts with impatience at their grief and hotly argues that the crucifixion of Jesus is a necessary good – if only they could see it – and something to celebrate along with a resurrection promised for centuries. {As they talk} the miles peel away. The couple ask the stranger to stay at their house when they reach the village ...

Commentary on Luke 24:13-35. *The Renovare Spiritual Formation Bible,* Richard J. Foster, ed. (HarperSanFrancisco, 2005), 1929; used with permission

Have you ever felt in times of despondency and despair that you are not alone but that someone, unrecognized, is walking beside you? In a few moments of contemplation, recall a few of the ways God has come to you both recognized and unrecognized and how you responded. Give thanks for that presence.

**PRAYER:** We do indeed, O God, give thanks for your presence. Our hearts are flooded with remembrance of both your presence and seeming absence. Though in times of absence we may have felt we were abandoned by you, it was not so. When the days of light returned we recognized your footprints walking with us in the most difficult of times. May we never lose the sense of being enfolded by your love and know that dreams postponed can be fulfilled in ways beyond our imaginings. We pray in the name of the One whose presence is always with us. Amen.

# WEDNESDAY, EASTER OCTAVE:
# THE AWAKENING

**Call to Awakening**

*As you gain ever more confidence in sensing the leadings of my Spirit, you will begin to see with new eyes, embrace the truths that are waiting for your understanding, and move joyfully toward the fulfillment of the tasks that are yours to accomplish.*

(Doctrine and Covenants 159:8)

**SCRIPTURE:** **Luke 24:28-32 At the Breaking of the Bread**

*When he was at table with them, he took bread, blessed, and broke it, and gave it to them. Then their eyes were opened, and they recognized him, and he vanished from their sight.*

**MEDITATION: The Story Continues**

The couple ask the stranger to stay at their house when they reach the village. One gets the image of a hooded man stooping through the doorway to sit at the table ... The stranger is asked to give the blessing. He picks up the bread, breaks it, passes it to Cleopas and Mary and in that glimpse of the way a friend always blessed and broke the bread, in that interstice of human and divine, a crack between heaven and earth, they see God. But it is only a glimpse. Then God is gone – but not gone. "*Were not our hearts burning within us while he was talking to us,*" they whisper. The broken hearts become the hearts that burn.

So we too can be surprised and blessed by the God who is expected, but rarely appears where and when and how we imagine. It is God's way to come cloaked, and also for his greatest promises to come cloaked. It is his way to come when the storm is peaking or fear deepest or when hope is almost gone or, if we are honest, utterly gone. No resurrection without Gethsemane. No Christmas Eve without a Good Friday. It is stitched into the fabric of thousands of years of the human race. But the other truth is that the world is interstitial – he will fling back his hood, he will throw off his robe, he will reveal his glory in those flashes of light between mortal and immortal, between the now and the forever ...Our task is not to figure everything out or imagine every angle God might come at us from, but to stay on the roads of our years, plodding on, encouraging one another with the voices and the mysteries of heaven. It is only that. To stay on the road until God in Disguise joins us and eventually comes to sit at our table. Or we at his.

*The Renovare Spiritual Formation Bible.* 1929-1930; used with permission

**Inviting Jesus into Our Homes**

The two traveling friends invite, indeed, press, the stranger to stay with them. "Be our guest," they say ... Jesus accepts the invitation to come into the home of his traveling companions, and he sits down at table with them ...There is bread on the table; there is wine on the table. The bread is taken, blessed, broken, and given. The wine is taken, blessed, and given. That is what happens around each table that wants to be a table of peace.

Every time we invite Jesus into our homes, that is to say, into our life with all its light and dark sides, and offer him the place of honor at our table, he takes the bread and the cup and hands them to us saying: "*Take and eat, this is my body. Take and drink, this is my blood. Do this to remember me.*" Are we surprised? Not really! Wasn't our heart burning when he talked to us on the road? Didn't we already know that he was not a stranger to us? Weren't we already aware that the one who was crucified by our leaders was alive and with us?

Henri J. M. Nouwen, *With Burning Hearts*
(Maryknoll, New York: Orbis Books, 1994),
59, 61, 66; used with permission

Now Let Our Hearts Within Us Burn
Now let our hearts within us burn As with a cleansing fire.
Your gracious Word has stirred in us A surge of new desire.
Should vision fail and courage yield To careless compromise,
Then redirect our falt'ring steps To braver enterprise.

As in another time and place, Along a forlorn road,
The Lord's renewing grace prevailed Till newborn courage glowed.
Our worship here has lifted us From self-indulgent care
And strengthened us to incarnate The priceless hope we share.

How can we now deny that voice That calls us from within,
Or blindly claim we need not bear Another's pain and sin?
In hearts that beat exultantly Renew your perfect will;
And send us forth again, Our mission to fulfill.

Geoffrey Spencer, *Hymns of the Saints,* No. 495

Have you ever, like the disciples on the road to Emmaus, been awakened to the fact that you were in the presence of the risen Lord? If so, what was that experience like for you?

**Times of Awakening**

Once on a visit to Sarasota, Florida I had occasion to visit the Ringling Museum. The museum was filled with remarkable and famous paintings. There was one, however, that captured my attention. It was a painting of that home in Emmaus at the very moment the two disciples recognized the Christ. The face of one disciple particularly reflected all: the awe, the amazement, the joy, the humility, the light of true awakening. Tears came to my eyes as I, too, experienced the marvel of that moment. I had been there. I knew that joy, that humility, that light. The experience has repeated itself over and over in my life so that I can truly say with Paul, "I know in whom I have believed."

On the night of Stephen Veazey's ordination to the office of prophet-president of the Community of Christ, I was sitting around a table with two good friends watching the event on television. As the hands – that wonderful mingling of hands – were laid on Stephen Veazey's head, the Spirit accompanying that moment did not confine itself to the Auditorium. It came right through the television into the room in which we were sitting and I am convinced into many rooms around the world. I felt I, too, was in the presence of the living Christ. That night in Emmaus was isolated to three people until the disciples ran to Jerusalem to tell their story. Through modern technology the Spirit is not limited by one place or time but can touch millions in the same instant. Perhaps that is what Jesus meant when he said to his disciples, "*Very truly I tell you, the one who believes in me will also do the works that I do and in fact, will do greater works than these, because I am going to the Father*" (John 14:12). Jesus was limited by space and time but the Spirit given in his name knows no such limitations. Spirit and technology work hand in hand to spread the Word to the most isolated of God's people. What a blessing!

Velma Ruch

What has your burning heart been asking of you? What are you avoiding? Are you afraid or perhaps not completely clear about what the call is for you? Do you lack trust that the God who calls you will also empower you? If this is the case with you and in your heart of hearts you truly want to respond, pray that the Spirit will give you the courage to follow and then take the first step.

**PRAYER:** When our hearts burn, O God, we know your Spirit is working within us. We recognize your presence, but even more we know you are calling us to the fulfillment of some task. We feel on the verge of an understanding for which some expression is required, whether it is taking up anew a task we were about to desert, or finding the words you need to have spoken or challenging us to further sanctification of our lives, or whatever else you may desire of us. Those who are sensitive to the burning heart and act upon it we recognize as the spiritual giants in our midst. As we follow in your footsteps may we become like them. Amen.

# THURSDAY, EASTER OCTAVE: "GO AND TELL"

**Call to Mission**

*Also I heard the voice of the Lord, saying, Whom shall I send, and who will go for us? Then said I, Here am I; send me. And he said, Go and tell this people.*
(Isaiah 6:6-9 IV)

**SCRIPTURE:** **Luke 24:33-35 They Returned to Tell**
That same hour they got up and returned to Jerusalem.

**MEDITATION: The Challenge of the Burning Heart**

Everything has changed. The losses are no longer felt as debilitating; home no longer is an empty place. The two travelers who started their journey with downcast faces now look at each other with eyes full of new light. The stranger who had become friend has given them his spirit, the divine spirit of joy, peace, courage, hope, and love. There is no doubt in their minds: He is alive! Not alive as before, not as the fascinating preacher and healer from Nazareth, but alive as a new breath within them...They have become people with a new mission who, together, have something to say, something important, something urgent, something that cannot remain hidden, something that must be proclaimed ...

Communion is not the end. Mission is. Communion, that sacred intimacy with God, is not the final moment of the Eucharistic life. We recognized him, but that recognition is not just for us to savor or to keep as a secret. As Mary of Magdala, so too the two friends had heard deep in themselves the words "Go and tell." ..."Go and tell "

What you have heard and seen is not just for yourself. It is for the brothers and sisters and for all who are ready to receive it. Go, don't linger, don't wait, don't hesitate. Go.

Henri J. M. Nouwen, *With Burning Hearts*, 79-81; used with permission

*How beautiful upon the mountains are the feet of the messenger who announces peace, who brings good news, who announces salvation, who says to Zion, Your God reigns.*

Isaiah 52:8

Have you been such a messenger? What was it that impelled you to "go tell"? What is the story you have to share?

**PRAYER:** **Prayer of the Story Teller**

Father of the dust who breathed life
into the blood and bone of woman, child, man,
from Eden's Garden
to Abel, Cain and Abraham,
from prophet to beggar,
unwed mother to desert father,
from all of humanity you call us
to the poetry in the One Story.
Creator of earth and Heaven,

of stone and evening star,
of wind and water, field and flower,
tiny sparrow and even the sparrow's song,
may our legacy be the glory
in the telling of your story
as you told it to your Son
who in turn told it to us.

May we tell it to each other
as we turn and come full circle
in the reaching of our hands,
in the mending of our hearts.
When single voices falter
may we rise in song together
as we pray unto you, Father,
in the living of your Story.
Amen.

Phyllis Price, *Holy Fire* (Paulist Press, 1998)

# FRIDAY, EASTER OCTAVE: THE CHALLENGE OF WAITING

**The Promise of Waiting**

*Those who wait for the Lord shall renew their strength, they shall mount up with wings like eagles, they shall run and not be weary, they shall walk and not fain.*

(Isaiah 40: 31)

**SCRIPTURE: John 21:1-3 "I Am Going Fishing"**

*Gathered there together were Simon Peter, Thomas called the twin, Nathanael of Cana in Galilee, the sons of Zebedee, and two others of his disciples. Simon Peter said to them, "I am going fishing." They said to him, "We will go with you." They went out and got into the boat, but that night they caught nothing.*

**MEDITATION: Turning from Everything to Christ**

Seven men were sitting alone in a room pondering their situation. They had left all to join the one who came to them while they were busy tending to their fishing and said, "Follow me." They spent three amazing years walking with him the roads of Galilee. They had come to relate to him not just as friend but as Messiah. "*Who do you say that I am?*" Jesus once asked. Without hesitation Peter responded, "*You are the Messiah, the son of the living God.*" "*Flesh and blood,*" Jesus said, "*has not revealed this to you but my Father in heaven*" (Matthew 16:15-17). Then the unthinkable happened. Jesus was crucified on a cross and Peter who once was such an avid follower and true believer, in fear for his safety, denied him. Disillusioned in himself and in the promises of Jesus, Peter with the rest locked himself in a room "*for fear of the Jews.*" Then once again, the totally unexpected happened. The resurrected Jesus penetrated the locked room and stood among them, "*Peace be unto you,*" he said. To their astonishment he breathed on them and blessed them, "*Receive the Holy Spirit.*" Then was gone.

What now? What does one make of what was once so sure, then was lost and suddenly reappeared again? True, the disciples had been warned but they did not comprehend. Now in a state of wanting to believe, their weary spirits brooded over a past and present they could not understand and a future that looked unpromising indeed.

Can you imagine the restless seven sitting in a room with nothing to do, with a dim hope at best and no patience to wait it out? Peter broke the silence. "*I am going fishing.*" The others immediately responded, "*We are going with you.*" At least here was something to do even if it were far less than they originally hoped. They went. Even the fishing was a failure. They caught nothing. Then a man, at first unrecognized, called to them from the shore and said, "*Throw your nets on the other side of the boat.*" They did and the catch was beyond belief.

So many lives have relived this story in a multitude of ways. John Killinger wrote about it in his book, *Christ in the Seasons of Ministry.* It was a compilation of a series of lectures he had given in 1982 to ministers and students of the Princeton Institute of Theology. Writing of the disillusionment that is likely to happen to all of us some time in our ministry, he wrote,

> As part of the developmental cycle of the minister's life, it is most likely to happen during the difficult transition period from early to later middle age, when the minister is smack in the middle of reassessing his or her pilgrimage and deciding where it is likely to lead in the years that are left ...

What we are doing, you see, after the period of intense activity and achievement that characterizes early middle life, is stopping to reexamine the course we are on, and to decide whether the trip has been worth it. For some, this means coming to terms with the failure to achieve – with having spent all those years in the search for the Holy Grail, only to come up weary and exhausted with full realization that it is too late, that they will never find the Grail. Or, even worse, it means coming to suspect there is no Grail at all.

The circumstances [may be different for] different people. It isn't the same with all of us, and we should never sit in judgment on those who take a way we would not take. But it is still the story of Simon Peter and the engulfing waves (Matthew 14:25-33). Whether our doubt and hesitance are for a moment or for ten years, we say no to Christ – or at least, "Wait a minute, Jesus, I'm not so sure about this any more." We can't help it. It's simply the way things are when you're forty or fifty and the road you were on suddenly comes to a washout or else to a multiple forking where every road looks more promising than the one you were on.

The effect personally seems devastating. After all the years, all the discipleship, all the pasturing and preaching, to hit the soft shoulder of doubt, to feel the waves parting beneath your feet and have that sense of spiritual vertigo or emotional queasiness that comes with it – "Lord, who can stand?"...

That's it, isn't it? Another turning point in life, another transition period; and the only thing that saves us from going under the waves is the outstretched hand of the Master. "Here, child, get in the boat." "Here, son, daughter, there are more sheep to feed."...

In the end, what else is there? After the stormy night at sea or the toilsome night with no fish taken, we come in to the Christ of the open fire, with the fish quietly simmering in a pan, and feel again the excitement that has grabbed at our hearts all these years, ever since we were youngsters. We walk with him along the shore, skipping rocks and thinking of faraway places, and hear him ask, probing gently, "Do you love me?"

"Yes, Lord, you know I do."

"Feed my sheep."

You can resist a scene like that? I can't. I turn from everything to Christ.

John Killinger, *Christ in the Seasons of Ministry* (Waco, Texas: Word Books, 1981), 64-67; used with permission

**PRAYER:** It is in finding Christ, Lord,
that we find the world and ourselves.
Reach out to us now,
in our stormy situations,
and take us by the hand.
Bring us back to the boat with
new commitment,
For yours is the gift of life.
Amen.

John Killinger

# SATURDAY, EASTER OCTAVE: BY THE SEASHORE

**The Call to Love**

*"This is my commandment that you love one another as I have loved you".*
(John 15:12)

**SCRIPTURE:** **John 21:4-19 "Do You Love Me?"**
*When they had finished breakfast, Jesus said to Simon Peter, "Simon, son of John, do you love me more than these?"*

**MEDITATION: Simon and Jesus**

A charcoal fire glows on the shore. Our gospel companions have been fishing all night. a fishing expedition initiated by Peter. Jesus calls to them, asking if they have caught any fish. They have caught nothing. "*Cast the net to the other side of the boat, and you will find some,*" he replies. So they cast the net and find it too full to haul in. John now recognizes the one standing on the shore. "*It is the Lord!*" he shouts. With sudden joy and relief, Simon grabs his tunic, jumps into the lake water, and swims to shore. The smell of fish roasting on the charcoal fire greets him as he wades out of the water, along with a kind proposal: "*Come and have breakfast,*" Jesus says ...

After breakfast he asks Simon Peter to walk with him along the shore. Jesus opens the conversation: "*Simon son of John, do you love me more than these?*" Simon replies, "*Yes, Lord; you know that I love you.*" Jesus asks this disciple a second time, "*Simon, son of John, do you love me?*" ... Then Jesus asks again, a third time, ...This insistent questioning finally gets through Simon's rough exterior and finds its way into the great soul and heart of this man. Peter begins to feel pain; the pain of not always being able to succeed – even as a fisherman: the pain of knowing he did not measure up to the gracious holiness that permeated the being of Jesus; the pain of knowing he had boasted of great loyalty to the Messiah but at the hint of threat had denied knowing him. Finally, he is able to stay with his pain and just to be with himself –human, weak, fallible, limited, sinful. Jesus had stayed with him all across these years and walks beside him now – just as he is. "*Lord, you know everything. You know that I love you.*"

Wendy J. Miller, *Jesus Our Spiritual Director* (Upper Room Books, 2004), 191-192

**On the Frontier with the Disciples**

We have been through a journey with a few of the disciples recovering from the intermingling of joy and pain following the crucifixion and the resurrection. The strands of pain and joy cannot easily be separated. For the disciples it was a process in which Jesus asked them to adjust to a new relationship. Though they were warned about this shift they either could not or did not initially respond. In our spiritual growth as well it is easy to overlook the warning signs, the nudges to a new life. It is easier to stay in the perceived comfort of the known. But Christ calls us to risk on new vision. True, it is dangerous out there. We can so easily succumb to betrayal of that which we most cherish and decide to take up accustomed habits, "*I will go fishing,*" said Peter. But out there on the frontier is where the disciples found themselves on Pentecost. It is where a prophet will always find himself or herself. It is where a prophetic people must be if we are to respond to the words, "*Follow me.*"

The journey ahead of us is not an easy one, but it is a journey to spiritual maturity. It is for this journey we were created. It is the fulfillment of the promise that we are that we might have joy.

**PRAYER:**

We are nothing without you, O Lord,
and it is hard to be something
when one is nothing.
It is hard to keep moving,
hard to keep pumping,
hard to keep giving out,
without you.
Come back to our lives in strength.
Renew the Spirit within us.
Give us bread for our wildernesses
For you are the Christ,
the Son of the Living Godl
Amen

John Killinger.

# SECOND WEEK OF EASTER
## THEME: A NEW CREATION: LESSONS FROM THE MASTER

**Seed of Promise**

*So if anyone is in Christ, there is a new creation, everything old has passed away, see, everything has become new.*

(2 Corinthians 5:17-21)

---

# THE SECOND SUNDAY OF EASTER: THE INCARNATIONAL LIFE

**Call to Discipleship**

*Therefore, since we are surrounded by so great a cloud of witnesses, let us also lay aside every weight and the sin that clings so closely, and let us run with perseverance that race which is set before us, looking to Jesus the pioneer and perfecter of our faith, who for the sake of the joy that was set before him endured the cross, disregarding the shame, and has taken his seat at the right hand of the throne of God.*

(Hebrews 12:1-2)

**SCRIPTURE:** **John 1:1-14 The Word Became Flesh**

*In the beginning was the Word and the Word was with God, and the Word was God…He came to what was his own, and his own people did not receive him. But to all who received him, who believed in his name, he gave power to become the children of God …*

*And the Word became flesh and lived among us, and we have seen his glory as the Father's only Son, full of grace and truth.*

**Doctrine and Covenants 28:9a All Things Are Spiritual**

*"Verily I say unto you that all things to me are spiritual."*

**MEDITATION: The Incarnational Tradition**

The Incarnational Tradition concerns itself with the relationship between spirit and matter. In short, God is manifest to us through material means.

Now, the spiritual and the material are not in opposition to one another, but are complementary. Far from being evil, the physical is meant to be inhabited by the spiritual. We are created so as to receive life from God, who is spirit, and to express that life through our bodies and in the physical world in which we live. The material world is created, in part, so as to make visible and manifest the realm of invisible spirit …

The specifically religious dimension is most fully expressed in our corporate worship. Here we use the physical and the material to express and manifest the spiritual. .

…Our task in liturgy is to glorify God in the various aspects of our worship life. We are to let the reality of God shine through the human or physical forms. This is true whether we are singing hymns or burning candles, dancing in ecstatic praise or bowing in speechless adoration ... We see, we smell, we touch, we taste, we hear. We absorb the faith by reliving the gospel and the passion in the liturgy. In short, God is manifest to us through material means ...

All of us are called to sacramental living. Redeemed by God through Christ, we are indwelt by the Holy Spirit and experience a growing transformation of character as our bodies come into a working harmony with our spirit. Hence our embodied self becomes a habitation of the Holy – a tabernacle – where we learn throughout our daily activities to function in cooperation with and in dependence upon God. Through time and experience we discover that everywhere we go is "holy ground" and every thing we do is "sanctified action." The jagged line dividing the sacred and the secular becomes very dim indeed, for we know that nothing is outside the realm of God's purview and loving care.

From Richard J. Foster, "The Incarnational Tradition" in *Streams of Living Water* (HarperSanFrancisco, 1998), 260-262, 272; used with permission

**Seeing God**

(In Truman Capote's autobiographical short story *A Christmas Memory*, an aging friend shares a revelation with her young companion while flying kites on Christmas morning)

"I always thought a body would have to be sick and dying before they saw the Lord. And I imagined that when he came it would be like looking at the Baptist window: pretty as colored glass with the sun pouring through, such a shine you don't know it's getting dark. And it's been a comfort to think of that shine taking away all the spooky feeling. For I'll wager it never happens. I'll wager at the very end a body realizes the Lord has already shown himself. That things as they are" – her hands circle in a gesture that gathers clouds and kites and grass and Queenie pawing earth over her bone – "just what they've always seen was seeing him. As for me I could leave the world with today in my eyes."

Published in *Alive Now* (November/December 1994)

**SCRIPTURE:** **Colossians 3:12-17 Clothe Yourselves with Love**

*As God's chosen ones, holy and beloved, clothe yourselves with compassion, kindness, humility, meekness, and patience ... Above all, clothe yourselves with love which binds everything together in perfect harmony. And let the peace of Christ rule in your hearts, to which indeed you were called in the same body.*

**Not I, But Christ in Me**

God's aim in the Christian life is to form Christ in us. From our side, there is nothing easy about this task. We turn away the very grace that would free us. Our "yes" to the gospel does not instantly make God our center, or love the source of our deeds. The competing loyalties that plague our divided hearts do not magically leave because we have chosen the path of the disciple. Loveless attitudes, misguided passions, and false images do not exit our lives because Christ has entered. The roots of sin and the patterns of our broken humanity are deeply embedded in the self. To know that we are for all time claimed by mercy is an unfathomable gift. But once this light has dawned, we are given the task of walking in the light. We are called to "grow into salvation" (1 Peter 2:2).

Growing into salvation is a mystery: it is fully a work of grace, and yet does not occur without our participation. It happens as we follow Jesus into all the twists and turns of life. God has chosen in this way to honor our personhood. The purpose of this journey is that having been saved by grace, we may go on to learn to cooperate with grace. Having entered the river of divine love, we must now learn how to swim with the current. We have begun the transforming process our ancestors called sanctification, the process by which the Holy Spirit renews our lives as we continue in the Way of Jesus.

Anthony Chvala Smith, *Understanding the Way*
(Herald House, 2003), 52

**PRAYER:** Transforming God, we know no higher longing in our lives than to abide in you as you abide in us. We strive to emulate the qualities you revealed in your life, but we know that is not enough. We seek to have an intimacy with you that sends the beams of your love right through us and shines its light on all we do. We wish to carry your presence with us at all times and pray that we may never lose the way to that inner source of love. It is in our longing for that Spirit, we pray. Amen

# THE SECOND MONDAY OF EASTER: LESSONS OF SURRENDER AND SUBMISSION

**A Reminder**

There lives more faith in honest doubt
Believe me, than in half the creeds.

Alfred Tennyson, *In Memoriam*

**SCRIPTURE:** **John 20:24-29 Thomas**

*"Unless I see the mark of the nails in his hands, and put my finger in the mark of the nails and my hand in his side, I will not believe."*

**MEDITATION: Surrender Through Love**

Like Thomas, at times, we, too, find ourselves locked in doubt, sadly refusing joy's entry into our life. This locked-in-ness is a subtle phenomenon, a gradual giving way to insecurities and self-doubt from which springs a fundamental demand for proofs and miraculous intervention. We put on blinders and say, "Show me!" ...

It was into the midst of the anguish and loneliness of doubt that Christ suddenly appeared to Thomas. It is in the midst of our woundedness that Christ continues to be a healing Easter presence. Amazingly, it was the blinding doubt of Thomas that served the function of making known to the world the wonder of God's merciful love. His skeptical bargaining was met with unconditional acceptance by Jesus. Jesus did not rebuke Thomas. He accepted him totally, going so far as to invite him to satisfy his appetite for proof. By putting his hand into the wound in his side, his finger into the wounds of his hands and feet, Thomas' heart was instantly overwhelmed with the awareness of the magnitude of Christ's gentleness and understanding. Pierced through with such love, Thomas knew; he knew with the knowledge of the Spirit:

*"My Lord, and my God!"*

In his act of surrender, the wounds of doubt, like agonizing boils, are first pierced then healed by Jesus' love. Thomas became whole in the strength of conviction and commitment. Once again power was made perfect in weakness (2 Cor. 12:9).

Bergan and Schwan, *Freedom*, 78-79

**SCRIPTURE:** **John 21:18-24 Peter**

*[Jesus said to Peter] "very truly I tell you, when you were younger you used to fasten your own belt and to go wherever you wished. But when you grow old, you will stretch out your hands, and some one else will fasten a belt around you and take you where you do not wish to go." (He said this to indicate the kind of death by which he would glorify God.) After this he said to him, "Follow me."*

*When Peter saw [John], he said to Jesus, "Lord, what about him?" Jesus said to him, "If it is my will that he remain until I come, what is that to you? Follow me!"*

**MEDITATION: "What Is That to You?"**

We believe it was the very John who was on the seashore that memorable day with Peter and Jesus and the rest who is recording this story. According to the account, John was following Peter and Jesus when they had that transforming conversation, "*Peter, do you love me?*" "*Yes, Lord, you know I do.*" "*Follow me.*" Did John overhear or did Peter tell him? If so, he was aware of the rest of the conversation as well. After being assured that the new Peter had grown in stature sufficient to become the pastoral head of the community, Jesus went one step further and indicated that the promise Peter had once made, "*I will lay down my life for you,*" would indeed be fulfilled. Peter took this news seemingly with acquiescence and without fear. Love involves responsibility and it always involves sacrifice. We know that Peter did die on a cross in Rome, crucified upside down for he felt unworthy to die as his Lord had died.

Peter, after this news, wondered about the fate of John, his fellow disciple. "Lord, what about him?" Jesus answered, "*If it is my will that he remain until I come, what is that to you? Follow me.*" John indeed lived a very long life and died in Ephesus seemingly surrounded by followers who learned from him. It was the last part of the statement that Jesus made, however, that has most significance for us: "... *what is that to you? Follow me.*" Sometimes we get so taken up with comparing our journey to that of others that we forget to focus on our own task and mission. We open ourselves to jealousy and envy and create stumbling blocks for ourselves by becoming upset over the actions of others. It is the spiritual discipline of submission that comes into focus here. Our concern is not with the actions or attitude or opportunities of others, difficult as they may be to bear some times, but with the call that has come to us and the challenge that is ours and ours alone.

William Barkley has written about this significant story:

> It was not for nothing that John recorded this incident. He recorded it to show Peter as the great shepherd of Christ's people. It may be, indeed it was inevitable, that people would draw comparisons in the early church. Some would say that Paul was the great one, for he fared to the ends of earth for Christ, but this chapter says that Peter, too, had his place. He might not write and think like John; he might not voyage and adventure like Paul; but he had the great honor, and the lovely task of being the shepherd of the sheep of Christ. And here is where we can follow in the steps of Peter. We may not be able to think like John; we may not be able to go to the ends of the earth like Paul; but each of us can guard someone else from going astray, and each of us can feed the lambs of Christ with the food of the word of Cod.
>
> *The Gospel of John* (Philadelphia: The Westminster Press, 1975), 286

Do you have the tendency to compare yourself with others and suffer when you cannot be like them or have the opportunities they have? On the other hand, are there times when others' actions so upset you that you may create turmoil in an entire congregation by your words and actions against them? What does the discipline of submission mean to you? How do you attempt to practice it?

**PRAYER:** Loving God, we have learned so much from those who preceded us about your presence and challenge to them in the midst of their pain and doubt and struggle. We have known that presence, too, and are deeply grateful for it. In humility and faith we pray that you will enlighten our minds to see, our heart to respond and our will to follow. It is in faith in the living Christ we pray. Amen.

# THE SECOND TUESDAY OF EASTER: A LESSON OF HUMILITY AND SERVICE

**Humility in Service**

*No one can assist in this work, except he shall be humble and full of love, having faith, hope, and charity, being temperate in all things whatsoever shall be entrusted to his care.*

( Doctrine and Covenants 11:4b)

**SCRIPTURE:** **John 13:1-20 Setting an Example**

*"Do you know what I have done to you? – You call me Teacher and Lord – and you are right, for that is what I am. So if I, your Lord and Teacher, have washed your feet, you also should wash one another's feet. For I have set you an example, that you also should do as I have done to you."*

**MEDITATION: A Basin, Some Water, and a Towel**

A basin, some water, and a towel – ordinary means to serve an extraordinary love!

Jesus' extravagant love for his disciples motivated the gentle and humble act of washing their feet. This deliberate action by Jesus also spoke of the profound level of awareness he had of his impending death ...

This incident is one of the most tender in the Gospels. Washing his disciples feet was for Jesus, and for them, an intimate moment of transparent vulnerability and surrender. Not even the evil intent active within Judas could destroy its spirit of goodness.

This simple, human gesture not only gave expression to the love which had grown between Jesus and his disciples throughout the years of the public ministry, but also represented the disciples' initiation into their own mature ministry without their master's physical presence.

"*I have given you an example so that you may copy what I have done in you.*"

...Wrapping a towel around his waist in the manner of a slave, he, the master and Lord, voluntarily submitted himself to the radicalness of a love that serves. In this reversal of roles, Jesus called his disciples also to become willing servants of love, even to the point of laying down *their* lives for others.

So wonderful was his act of love that Peter and the others would be able to comprehend the full import of it only after Jesus' death and resurrection.

...A basin, some water, and a towel had become for the disciples, and for us, a powerful prophetic symbol of the wholeness of Jesus' life, death, resurrection, and ascension – the wholeness of his love.

Jaqueline Syrup Bergan and S. Marie Schwan, *Surrender: A Guide for Prayer.* (Winona, Minnesota: Christian Brothers Publications, 1986), 43-44

**PRAYER:** Jesus, you asked the disciples once if they could drink of the cup you were called to drink. Though they answered "yes" they did not necessarily know what they were saying. We have said "yes" too, and in times of struggle we are not always so sure we meant it. Give us strength, O God, to follow where you lead and the love to minister "to the least of these." We pray in humility and in submission to your will in us. Amen.

# THE SECOND WEDNESDAY OF EASTER: A LESSON IN LOVE

**A New Commandment**

*"I give you a new commandment, that you love one another. Just as I have loved you, you also should love one another. By this everyone will know that you are my disciples, if you have love for one another".*

(John 13:34-35)

**SCRIPTURE:** **Romans 8:35, 37-39 Nothing Can Separate Us from Christ's Love**

*Who will separate us from the love of Christ? Will hardship, or distress, or persecution, or famine, or nakedness, or peril, or sword?...No, in all these things we are more than conquerors through him who loved us. For I am convinced that neither death, nor life, nor angels, nor rulers, nor things present, not things to come, nor powers, nor height, nor depth, nor anything else in all creation, will be able to separate us from the love of God inChrist Jesus, our Lord.*

**Book of Mormon, Moroni 7:52-53 Cleave to Charity**

*"Wherefore, cleave to charity, which is the greatest of all, for all things must fail; but charity is the pure love of Christ, and it endures forever and whoever is found possessed of it at the last day, it shall be well with him. "Wherefore, my beloved brethren, pray to the Lord with all energy of heart that you may be filled with this love which he has bestowed upon all who are true followers of his Son, Jesus Christ, that you may become the sons of God, that when he shall appear, we shall be like him, (for we shall see him as he is) that we may have this hope, that we may be purified even as he is pure."*

**1 John 4:7-12 Children of God**

*Dear friends, let us love one another, because love is from God. Everyone who loves is a child of God and knows God, but the unloving know nothing of God. For God is love, and God's love was disclosed to us in this, that he sent his only son as the remedy for the defilement of our sins. If God thus loved us, dear friends, we in turn are bound to love one another. God...dwells in us if we love one another.*

**Ephesians 3:18-19 Filled With The Fullness of God**

*I pray that you may have the power to comprehend, with all the saints, what is the breadth and length and height and depth, and to know the love of Christ that surpasses knowledge, so that you may be filled with all the fullness of God.*

**MEDITATION: Love with Skin on It**

The most wonderful thing that can happen to any human being is to be loved. It alone speaks to the gnawing sense of insignificance and isolation we feel. And the marvelous news is that we have been loved and we are loved, each and every one of us. uniquely and individually. At the heart of the universe is love, divine love, personal, intimate God-love for you and for me. We are known! We are chosen! We are loved! Once experienced at the deepest levels of the soul, no reality can be more profoundly disturbing, more radically healing, more utterly transforming ...

Maybe, just maybe, our universe is populated in ways we can hardly imagine. Maybe what we call empty space is not empty at all but teeming with life and love and God's animating presence throughout. Maybe, just maybe, behind all things is real intelligence: intelligence that is wholly personal; intelligence that is wholly other than us but that also has freely chosen to be involved in the affairs of this universe – and, in fact, at one pinpoint in human history, did indeed become so intimately involved as to be incarnated as a baby, a baby who grew to be a man and lived like no one ever lived and died like no one ever died. All so we could see love with skin on it. And then this man rose from the dead so we could know that this One who is Love lives on eternally, and that we can participate in his life, loving and being loved, now and forever.

Richard J. Foster in James Bryan Smith, *Embracing the Love of God* (HarperSanFrancisco, 1995), xiii-xv; used with permission

**What Do I Love When I Love You?**

Nothing can compare to the experience that comes to us when Christ far from being an abstraction becomes a reality in our lives. Augustine in his *Confessions* wrote of the long period of time when he longed for Christ but still closed him out and then of the joy he experienced when his eyes were opened and he truly saw:

> Too late have I loved you, O Beauty so ancient and so new, too late have I loved you! Behold, you were within me, while I was outside... You were with me, but I was not with you...You have called to me and have cried out, and have shattered my deafness. You have blazed forth with light, and have shone upon me, and you have put my blindness to flight! You have sent forth fragrance and I have drawn in my breath, and I pant after you. I have tasted you, and I hunger and thirst after you. You have touched me, and I have burned for your peace.

Augustine, *The Confessions of Saint Augustine*, John K. Ryan, trans. (New York: Image Doubleday, 1960), 254

Then Augustine went on to try to describe what this association with God was like:

> What is it, then, that I love when I love you? Not bodily beauty and not temporal glory, not the clear, shining light, lovely as it is to our eyes, not the soft smell of flowers and ointments and perfumes, not manna and honey, not limbs made for the body's embrace, not these do I love when I love my God. Yet I do love a certain light, a certain voice, a certain odor, a certain food, an embrace for the man within me, where his light, which no place can contain floods into my soul; where he utters words that time does not speed away; where he sends forth an aroma that no wind can scatter; where he provides food that no eating can lessen; where he so clings that satiety does not sunder us. This is what I love when I love my God.

*Confessions,* 233-234

**PRAYER:**

Lord my God, when your love spilled over
into creation
You thought of me.
I am
from love of love for love.
Let my heart, O God, always
recognize,
cherish,
and enjoy your goodness in all of creation.
Direct all that is me toward your praise.
Teach me reverence for every person, all things.
Energize me in your service.
Lord God
may nothing ever distract me from your love
neither health nor sickness
wealth nor poverty
honor nor dishonor
long life nor short life.

May I never seek nor choose to be other
than You intend or wish. Amen.

Bergan and Schwan, *Freedom,* 12;
used with permission

# THE SECOND THURSDAY OF EASTER: A LESSON IN INDIVIDUALITY

**The Art of Becoming**

*And all of us, with unveiled faces, seeing the glory of the Lord as though reflected in a mirror, are being transformed into the same image from one degree of glory to another; for this comes from the Lord, the Spirit.*

(2 Corinthians 3:18)

**SCRIPTURE:** **Genesis 1:26-27 Made in the Image of God**

*"Let us make humankind in our image, according to our likeness ..."*
*So God created humankind in his image, in the image of God he created them; male and female he created them.*

**John 14:1-3 "There Are Many Dwelling Places"**

*"In my Father's house there are many dwelling places. If it were not so, would I have told you that I go to prepare a place for you?"*

**Isaiah 43:1 "I Have Called You By Name"**

*"But now, thus says the Lord, he who created you, O Jacob, he who formed you, O Israel: Do not fear, for I have redeemed you; I have called you by name, you are mine."*

**John 17:11 "May They Be One"**

*"Holy father, protect them in your name that you have given me, so they may be one as we are one."*

**MEDITATION: Image and Likeness**

The early church fathers, taking some liberty with the literal interpretation of the statement from Genesis that we are created in the image and likeness of God saw "image" as expressing our human potential and "likeness" as fulfillment, the actualization of that potential. In this sense human development is a journey from the image of God toward the likeness of God. This fulfillment Jung called "individuation," which suggests that the process toward "likeness" will not necessarily be the same for each individual. The emphasis is on a development in which each of us can become the best of who we are.

Velma Ruch, *The Transforming Power of Prayer*, Vol. 1
(Herald House, 1999), 119

**Individuality in Community**

It is interesting to consider that very diverse group that Jesus had chosen as his disciples and who were assembled with him in the upper room that crucial night. They were full of questions, of affirmations and doubts. Jesus, who knew them all intimately and loved them in their diversity, tenderly dealt with each one according to his need. At one point, sensing consternation in the group, Jesus moves to heal, as he does so often that memorable evening. "*Do not let your hearts be troubled,*" he says, "*In my Father's house there are many dwelling places. I go to prepare a place for you.*" Whether we refer to that place as "room" or "dwelling place" or "mansion," it all comes down to the fact that in all of our differences there is a place made especially for each of us where we are home, where we belong. There is a place for Peter, for Philip, for Thomas, for you, and for me. That place, often thought to be ours after we die, is not on hold until then. It is for now. It is available for habitation at the point we discover an open door with a welcome sign on it and we walk into the home we have dreamed of for so long. All our longing, all our homesickness has led us to the place where we belong, where we have peace, where we know fullness of life.

It is important for us to recognize that experiencing "fullness of life" is not the same for each of us. Dante, in his pilgrim journey recounted in *The Divine Comedy* made that very clear as he journeyed through the spheres of Paradise. He had already experienced Hell and Purgatory. Now, being led by his beloved Beatrice, he had come to Paradise. There he discovered to his amazement that there was a hierarchy of glories that paradoxically was not a hierarchy. The whole was arranged so that each spirit received the fullness that would complete what that person found most satisfying. Dante paused to ask one of the spirits in "the lower" sphere if she didn't yearn to be up "higher." Her answer is famous, "Our peace in his will."

But there is a corollary that goes along with the importance of individual uniqueness. We are created so that we can be an important asset to community.

That is what Jesus meant when he prayed that "*they may be one as we are one.*" The body of Christ, as Paul spoke of it, consisted of individual members, a multitude of organs, each with its own function and importance. If one failed to work properly the whole body suffered. Each was important to the success of the whole. Even the "weak," who might need a little more support were crucial to the body.

Milton uses architecture to express the same idea. In *Areopagitica* he writes,

> While the temple of the Lord was building, some cutting, some squaring the marble, others hewing the cedars, there should be a sort of irrational men who could not consider there must be many schisms, and many dissections made in the quarry and in the timber, ere the house of God can be built. And when every stone is laid artfully together, it cannot be united into a continuity, it can but be contiguous in this world; neither can every piece of the building be of one form; nay, rather the perfection consists in this, that out of many moderate varieties and brotherly dissimilitudes that are not vastly disproportional, arises the goodly and the graceful symmetry that commends the whole pile and structure. Let us, therefore, be more considerate builders, more wise in spiritual architecture, when great reformation is expected.

> We enter the body of Christ as living temples eager to add our individuality and beauty to the whole. It will be the Spirit moving among us that will be the *architect* who can create unity out of diversity and create a relationship of power. In this relationship each member has value and is sent out on a mission of healing and redemption.

**PRAYER:** God of all people, all races and nations, we thank you for our personal uniqueness. We glory in who we are and you have created us to strive to be the best that we can be. But alone, O God, we are not complete. We need you and one another. Help us as we try to create the peaceable kingdom in your name. We pray for our own sakes and for the world. Amen.

# THE SECOND FRIDAY OF EASTER: PEACE TO THE TROUBLED

**Prayer in Time of Need:**

*Hear my cry; O God; listen to my prayer. From the end of the earth I call to you, when my heart is faint. Lead me to the rock that is higher than I; for you are my refuge, a strong tower against the enemy. Let me abide in your tent forever, find refuge under the shelter of your wings*

(Psalm 61:1-4).

**SCRIPTURE:** **John 14:25-28 Do Not Be Afraid**

*"Do not let your hearts be troubled and do not let them be afraid."*

**Matthew 11:28 Take My Yoke upon You**

*"Come to me all you that are weary and are carrying heavy burdens; and I will give you rest. Take my yoke upon you, and learn from me; for I am gentle and humble in heart and you will find rest for your souls. For my yoke is easy, and my burden is light."*

**MEDITATION: The Shadow of the Cross**

The night before his crucifixion Jesus met in an upper room with his disciples. He was deeply concerned about them and the agony they would experience in the next few days. Full of concern and love for them he said, "*Do not let your hearts be troubled and do not let them be afraid.*"These words came out of Jesus' experience just a few days before when some Greeks came and offered him a way out of the coming crucifixion. The cost of following the road he was on for a moment seemed formidable, "*Now is my soul troubled,*" he said, "*And what should I say – Father, save me from this hour?" "No, it is for this reason that I have come to this hour. Father, glorify your name.*"Jesus could have saved his life but it would have meant a denial of his vocation.

He trusted the Father enough to be willing to walk the way of Gethsemane and the Cross.

Jesus wasn't sure how well his disciples would fare when darkness descended upon them. He wanted to lead them to a trust that would uphold them in the dark times.

"*Believe in God, believe also in me,*" he said. So often we, as present-day disciples, don't let that advice and promise penetrate our being. As we walk up the Worshipers' Path in the Temple, happy in the beauty and light and joy of being found, there looms before us the shadow of a cross. We slow down, we hesitate, we do not want to enter that shadow. But enter it we do whether we want to or not. Very often after the mountaintop, we find ourselves in the shadow of the valley of death and ask, How could this happen to me? Then we focus on Gethsemane and recognize how close that suffering, praying figure is to our own sorrow and need.

We have to admit that the darkness of spirit that comes to the most dedicated is very difficult to bear. We hear it in Christ's cry on the cross, "*My God, My God, why have you forsaken me?*" We hear it in the Psalmist, "*O my God, I cry by day, but you do not answer; and by night, but find no rest*" (Psalm 22:2). We hear it in Job: "*And now my soul is poured out within me; days of affliction have taken hold of me. The night racks my bones, and the pain that gnaws me takes no rest. I cry to you and you do not answer me; I stand, and you merely look at me"* (Job 30:16, 17, 20). We do everything we know and still nothing. George Buttrick expressed it, "It feels we are beating on heaven's door with bruised knuckles in the dark."

The most difficult part of this darkness is the seeming abandonment by the one who has loved us and whom we have loved in return. Some of the saddest lines I know in poetry were spoken by Samson in Milton's *Samson Agonistes*:

> I was his nursling once and choice delight,
> His destin'd from the womb...
> He led me on to mightiest deeds...
> But now hath cast me off as never known.

Yet Samson, as did Job and the psalmist and all the rest discovered that pain was not the end of the story, that God had not abandoned them after all.

Learning to wait and to trust is important. Neither the life nor the healing that can come to us is likely to be immediate. The God of the Bible, someone has said, is a God of deliverance, but more often a God of blessing. Miracles do occur in which healing and release come instantly. More often it is a gradual process in which we need to train ourselves to be patient and be aware of change, gradual though it may be.

Christ revealed to us the redemptive possibilities in life's extremities. In his earthly ministry he came to people at the point of their greatest need. Even on the cross he reached out to the repentant thief, "*Today you will be with me in Paradise.*" If we wish to participate in Christ's resurrection and the joy that accompanies it, we must also participate in his suffering. That suffering emerged from love, from bearing the sins of the world. As Christ's disciples we cannot rationalize an escape from carrying the burdens of others. We need to find the beauty possible when we love one another.

To each of us who stand in need of healing from the wounds of life Jesus says, "*Come unto me, all ye that labor and are heavy laden, and I will give you rest.*" That is the discovery that gives meaning to life and allows us to put our dreams and hopes on the altar and pray. "Lord, let thy will be done in me." When we do we may find what it is to "rise triumphant through the sacrament of pain." Though we may still be in the valley of the shadow, we will fear no evil for we are accompanied by a love that has known its own sacrifice and extends to us a nail-pierced hand to lead us out of the shadow into the light of the Resurrection. The journey through the shadow of the cross is a journey to the heart of love, to that wounded healer who died that we might have life and have it more abundantly.

Velma Ruch, "The Cross Life: The Spirituality of the Wounded Healer,"
in *Summoned to Pilgrimage* (Herald House, 1994)

**PRAYER:** O God, you who so loved the world that you gave your only begotten Son that whoso believed on him would not perish but have everlasting life, in our need we cry out to you, "Must this cup be mine?" Give us the strength to bear the burdens that are ours and to grow in understanding of your will in us. May we, like so many before us, rise radiant in the sacrament of pain. Amen.

# THE SECOND SATURDAY OF EASTER: THE BLESSING

**The Power of Prayer**

*Ask, and it will be given you; search, and you will find; knock, and the door will be opened for you. For everyone who asks receives, and everyone who searches finds, and for everyone who knocks, the door will be opened.*

(Matthew 7:7-8)

**SCRIPTURE:** **John 17 (excerpts). Jesus Prays with the Disciples**

*Father, the hour has come, glorify your Son so that the Son may glorify you.*

*This is eternal life, that they may know you, the only true God and Jesus Christ whom you have sent.*

*I have made your name known to those whom you gave me from the world. They were yours and you gave them to me and they have kept your word . . . I am asking on their behalf; I am not asking on behalf of the world but on behalf of those whom you gave me, because they are yours.*

*Holy Father, protect them in your name that you have given me, so they may be one as we are one.*

*Sanctify them in the truth; your word is truth. As you have sent me into the world, so I have sent them into the world. And for their sakes I sanctify myself, so that they also may be sanctified in truth.*

*I ask not only on behalf of these but also on behalf of those who will believe in me through their word, that they may all be one. As you, Father, are in me and I am in you, may they also be in us, so that the world will believe that you sent me.*

*I will make [your name] known, so that the love with which you have loved me may be in them and I in them.*

**MEDITATION:** Spend time in meditation on selected words from Jesus' prayer with and for his disciples. Jot down briefly thoughts that come to you.

*Father, the hour has come*

*This is eternal life that they may know you, the only true God and Jesus Christ whom you have sent.*

*I have made your name known to those you gave me from the world*

*Holy Father, protect them in your name that you have given me so they may be one as we are one.*

*As you have sent me into the world so I have sent them into the world*
*For their sakes I sanctify myself so they also may be sanctified in truth.*

*I ask not only in behalf of these but also on behalf of those who will believe in me through their word, that they may all be one.*

*I will make your name known so that the love with which you have loved me may be in them and I in them.*

**PRAYER:** O Lord, my God, and Jesus Christ, your Son, I was not with you in that upper room and the gathering in prayer afterwards, but I have felt the power as the timeless words resonated in my heart. In your presence I have touched the hem of your garment and have been lifted into the spheres of eternity. You have sent me into the world as you sent that small circle of disciples so long ago. I pray that I, too, may be empowered by your Spirit as I go forth in your name. Amen.

# THE THIRD WEEK OF EASTER
## THEME: WALKING IN THE SPIRIT

## THE THIRD SUNDAY OF EASTER: THE PROMISE OF THE HOLY SPIRIT

**The Invitation**

Come, Holy Spirit, come. Come Holy Spirit come.
As we lift this invitation, rest upon this congregation –
Holy Spirit, come. Come, Holy Spirit, come.

Vicky Vaughn, *Sing a New Song,* No. 6

**SCRIPTURE: John 14:15-17 Another Advocate**

*And I will ask the Father and he will give you another Advocate to be with you forever. This is the spirit of Truth which the world cannot receive because he neither sees him or knows him. You know him because he abides in you, and he will be in you.*

**Acts 2:38-39 The Gift of the Holy Spirit**

*Peter said to them, "Repent and be baptized every one of you in the name of Jesus Christ so that your sins may be forgiven; and you will receive the gift of the Holy Spirit. For the promise is for you, for your children, and for all who are far away, everyone whom the Lord our God calls to him.*

**MEDITATION: A Promise With Strings Attached**

Though all persons have the capacity for response to the Divine, deep spiritual communion is rare. A surprisingly large number of those who consider themselves religious and spend a substantial portion of their lives in church participation maintain they seldom, if ever, have had a direct experience with God. They know God by report and not by first-hand experience. One can share the beauty of scripture, participate in the ordinances of the church, and hear with joy the testimonies of others –but something is lacking. For faith to serve as the very foundation of our lives and become a means of transformation, we must personally know the reality of the Infinite and the power of intersection. Something must be burning brightly in us; a transforming experience must be at the center of our lives. Somewhere we must have participated in the presence of God in compelling power. In the words of Gerard Manley Hopkins, "I greet Him the days I meet Him/ And bless when I understand" (*The Wreck of the Deutschland,* pt.1, line 40).

Velma Ruch, *The Signature of God* (Herald House, 1986), 309

A very common reason for closing "the window of Divine surprise" is it cost. Full communion with God makes claims on the totality of our personhood. It requires humility, love, and the surrender of our wills. Such surrender is exceedingly difficult. We do not want a righteousness that can come to us only from God. We want to keep ourselves under our own control, make our own plans. Just as often we turn away to numb the longing of the "restless heart." The search may take place in darkness and our endurance of the mountains of the mind, "cliffs of fall/ Frightful, sheer, no man fathomed," as Gerard Manley Hopkins writes of them, is limited. We can stand it so long and then we strive to change our anxiety into a prosperous sense of normalcy, often by giving ourselves to the ritual of church-going, committee meetings, church drives, etc., and become accustomed through great activity to live in a cooled and slowed-down faith. We become "distracted from distraction by distraction" (T. S. Eliot, "Burnt Norton")

We need to recognize the distinction between action which is diverting and numbing and action born from a sense of communion with God.

*Signature of God*, 310-311

Jesus' promise of the presence of the Holy Spirit is not designed for a select few. It is for all of us, but the way of intersection must be primarily an individual adventure, sought and cultivated by those who recognize its importance, but who together with others of similar concern create a community in which intersection is experienced in corporate form. That was the experience at Pentecost.

**PRAYER:** I have known your presence, O God, in a multitude of ways and have been blessed by the wonder of your gracious giving. But the vessel I bring to you for filling is much too small. Sometimes my cup overflows because it is simply too small to hold the fullness of your desire in me. In the quiet moments of my life I recognize what I have lost through being unprepared to receive the immensity of your love. I ask your forgiveness and in this sacred moment offer you my whole heart for filling. Amen.

# THE THIRD MONDAY OF EASTER: WAYS OF THE SPIRIT

**Seed of Promise**

*And it shall come to pass in the last days, saith God, I will pour out of my Spirit upon all flesh, and your sons and your daughters shall prophesy, and your young men shall see visions, and your old men shall dream dreams. And on my servants and on my handmaidens I will pour out in those days of my Spirit and they shall prophesy.*

(Acts 2:17-18 IV)

**SCRIPTURE:** **Psalm 139:7-12 The Omnipresence of the Spirit**

*Where can I go from your spirit? Or where can I flee from your presence? If I ascend to heaven, you are there; if I make my bed in Sheol, you are there. If I take the wings of the morning and settle at the farthest limits of the sea, even there your hand shall lead me, and your right hand shall hold me fast. If I say, "Surely the darkness shall cover me, and the light around me become night" even the darkness is not dark to you; the night is as bright as the day, for darkness is as light to you.*

**Ezekiel 1:1-3; 2:1-3 Stand Up on Your Feet**

*In the thirtieth year in the fourth month, on the fifth day of the month, as I was among the exiles by the river Chebar, the heavens were opened, and I saw visions of God. On the fifth day of the month (it was the fifth year of the exile of King Jehoiachin), the word of the Lord came to the priest Ezekiel son of Buzi, in the land of Chaldeans by the river of Chebar; and the hand of the Lord was on him there.*

*He said to me: O mortal, stand up on your feet, and I will speak with you. And when he spoke to me, a spirit entered into me and set me on my feet; and I heard him speaking to me. He said to me, Mortal, I am sending you to the people of Israel, to a nation of rebels who have rebelled against me; they and their ancestors have transgressed against me to this day.*

**Luke 4:18-21 "The Spirit of the Lord Is upon Me"**

*The Spirit of the Lord is upon me, because he has anointed me to bring good news to the poor. He has sent me to proclaim release to the captives and recovery of sight to the blind, to let the oppressed go free, to proclaim the year of the Lord's favor."*

*...Then he began to say to them, "Today this scripture has been fulfilled in your hearing."*

**MEDITATION: The Pervasive and Invasive Action of the Spirit**

As members of the Community of Christ, we are a people who have taken very seriously an exploration into the workings of the Holy Spirit. Two significant beliefs of the Restoration affirm that all things are spiritual and that the Divine has never ceased to speak through prophets and ordinary people Both beliefs have to do with the Holy Spirit. Are they essentially the same thing or is there some difference at least in emphasis? Are the spiritual disciplines in which we engage the same for each or should we have a heightened awareness of disciplines that prepare us to be participants in the revelatory process?

In my thinking, incomplete as it is, I have divided the work of the Spirit into two categories: "pervasive and "invasive." The Spirit that pervades all of creation and allows us to recognize a sacramental universe to which we can relate I have called "pervasive." The revelatory Spirit that comes as a fire that burns within our hearts I have called "invasive." The distinction, I recognize, is somewhat artificial since one blends into the other, but it has merit. F. Henry Edwards has written, "There is the direct inspiration of the prophets and there is this pervasive and supporting inspiration which prepares the way and builds up understanding. Both are evidence of divine concern" (*The Edwards Commentary on the Doctrine and Covenants* [Herald House, 1986], 8).

The pervasive spirit is part of our very being. It is "*the light which is in all things which giveth life to all things which is the law by which all things are governed*" (D. and C. 85). The "direct inspiration" which may be given in different ways and for different purposes to both prophets and a prophetic people is an affirmation that the Spirit is more than divine energy which permeates us all. We engage in a One on one encounter that allows us to communicate on a very high level. As human beings made in the image of God we have within us not only the Spirit of God but the capacity to recognize the Spirit as it intersects our very being. Much of the recent emphasis on spiritual disciplines has been related to the "pervasive" aspect. Is it time that we seriously consider disciplines that relate particularly to the revelatory aspect and explore what they might be?

The invasive work of the Spirit belongs far more to the realm of the human than to non-human nature. The Spirit of God brooded over the waters of creation and all things were given life by its presence. Human beings are in a separate category, however. They were created in the image of God and meant to have communion with God's active presence. Scholars believe that the Old Testament name for Spirit, *ruach*, generally suggests energetic action on the part of God rather than the immanence of God simply pervading creation. Only into human beings did God transfer his own life force, his breath (see Kenneth Leech, *Experiencing God* [Harper and Row, 1985],60). In this context the energetic action of the Spirit represents an invasive rather than pervasive power. That is not to say that the pervasive power that makes our universe sacramental is not of great importance to us. It is rather to say that the Holy Spirit takes an active role in human lives. The self-consciousness of God comes in contact with the self-consciousness of the human. There is a direct and invasive encounter that to those who respond is life changing.

Many prophets and saints and ordinary people of past and present have given testimony to the reality of this experience. It happened to Isaiah in the temple whose lips were touched with fire; to Ezekiel who in a vision of fire was commanded to stand upon his feet so God could speak to him; to Jeremiah who could not give up his prophetic task because of the fire burning in his bones, to Paul on the road to Damascus when he was blinded by the light of Christ; to Samuel who heard the voice in the temple; to young Joseph as he knelt in the grove; to Mary confronted by the angel Gabriel; to Esther who came to the kingdom for such a time as this; to Enos who "hungered" for divine presence; to the brother of Jared as related in the story of the Jaredites in the Book of Mormon, and on an on. Though each responded in different ways according to the situation in which they found themselves, for all of them, it was an experience of sanctification, refining fire, and of life direction, a vocation.

Velma Ruch "The Church of Burning Hearts" (unpublished)

How have you experienced the Spirit? Do you respond more to the "pervasive" or "invasive" presence of the Spirit? If you can, think of experiences you have personally had in each of the categories. How did they come to you? Do you intentionally prepare yourself to receive? What spiritual disciplines are most helpful for you? Are there some you would like to learn more about?

**PRAYER:** You break into our lives, O God, in a multitude of ways. Our very lives are dependent upon your presence and we wish to truly become a temple where your Spirit may abide. Help us as we grow in our understanding of your way with us. Give us eyes to see and ears to hear. Sanctify us in your name and give us power to discern your will for us, we pray. Amen.

# THE THIRD TUESDAY OF EASTER: ILLUMINED BY THE SPIRIT

**Mysterious Presence**

Like dry flour, which cannot become one lump of dough, one loaf of bread, without moisture, we who are many could not become one in Christ Jesus without the water that comes down from heaven. And like parched ground, which yields no harvest unless it receives moisture, we who were once like a waterless tree could never have lived and borne fruit without this abundant rainfall from above.

(Irenaeus, Bishop of Lyons, c. 125-202)

**SCRIPTURE:** **John 4:23-24 "Worship in Spirit and in Truth"**

*But the hour is coming, and is now here; when the true worshipers will worship the Father in spirit and truth, for the Father seeks such as these to worship him. God is spirit, and those who worship him must worship in spirit and in truth.*

**Doctrine and Covenants 85:3a Light**

*And the light which now shineth which giveth you light, is through him who enlighteneth your eyes, which is the same light that quickeneth your understandings; which proceeded from the presence of God, to fill the immensity of space.*

**John 17:17-19 Becoming Sanctified in Truth**

*Sanctify them in the truth; your word is truth. As you have sent me into the world, so I have sent them into the world. And for their sakes I sanctify myself, so that they may be sanctified in truth.*

**MEDITATION: Repentance and Illumination**

Illumination as used in this context essentially means God present in our spirit. It is not a psychic phenomenon, a feeling dredged up from our subconscious, but the actual meeting of Divine with human. The operation of the Spirit in our lives may be manifold, but in whatever way it comes it is a power that works through us but is not from us; it is felt as something given for which we are not ourselves responsible. It may be as quiet and as normal as breathing, ever present, constantly sustaining life, assuring us that "The eternal God is our home and underneath are the everlasting arms." Or it may come as the Hound of Heaven that follows us down the labyrinthine ways even when we are trying to escape.

Not always, however, is the Reality known quite so tender. Illumination may come as a bolt of lightning and like Saul of Tarsus we may be stopped in our way and turned around to face a new direction. The action may cause great inner disturbance and even send us to Nineveh when we don't want to go there. The Spirit in lightning strength may be exceedingly painful but it can shatter our deafness and for the stubborn and unheeding it has the force to "break, blow, burn, and make us new."

Repentance and illumination are closely entwined. Illumination leads to repentance and repentance is blessed by illumination. How that works is beautifully illustrated by St. Bernard of Clairvaux who has been called the most brilliant religious genius of the twelfth century. At the end of his series of sermons *On the Song of Songs* he chose to tell of his own experience with Christ. It is a powerful and moving testimony of the operation of Christ's spirit in his life:

> You ask, then, how I knew that He was present, since His ways are past finding out" Because the Word is living and effective, and as soon as ever He has entered into me, He has aroused my sleeping soul, and stirred and softened and pricked my heart, that hitherto was sick and hard as stone ... My senses told me nothing of His coming. I knew that He was present only by the movement of my heart; I perceived His power because it put my sins to flight and exercised a strong control on all my impulses. I have been moved at His wisdom, too, uncovering my secret faults and teaching me to see their sinfulness; and I have experienced His gentleness...in the renewal...of my mind...I have beheld to some degree the beauty of His glory and have been filled with awe as I gazed at His manifold greatness (229-230).
>
> Velma Ruch, *The Signature of God*, 338-340

Bernard of Clairvaux was a great hymn writer as well. One of his best-loved hymns is included in *Hymns of the Saints*, No. 167:

Jesus, the very thought of thee
With sweetness fills my breast,
But sweeter far thy face to see,
And in thy presence rest.

No voice can sing, no heart can frame,
Nor can the mind recall
A sweeter sound than they blest name,
O Savior of us all.

O Hope of every contrite heart,
O Joy of all the meek,
To those that fall, how kind thou art!
How good to those who seek.

But what to those who find? Ah this
Nor tongue nor pen can show;
The love of Jesus, what it is
None but who love him know. Amen.

**PRAYER:** When kindled by Thy Spirit's light,
Our minds, illumed, more clearly see
That every good which in us is
Derives, Eternal One, from Thee. Amen

E. Y. Hunker, *Hymns of the Saints,* No. 282

# THE THIRD WEDNESDAY OF EASTER: EMPOWERED BY THE SPIRIT

**The Gift of the Spirit**

*When they had prayed, the place in which they were gathered together was shaken; and they were all filled with the Holy Spirit and spoke the word of God with boldness.*

(Acts 4:31)

**SCRIPTURE:** **Acts 1:8 Power through the Holy Spirit**

*But you will receive power when the Holy Spirit has come upon you; and you will be my witnesses in Jerusalem in all Judea and Samaria, and to the ends of the earth.*

**Doctrine and Covenants 154:7a,b "My Spirit Will Be with You"**

*If you will move out in faith and confidence to proclaim my Gospel my Spirit will empower you and there will be many who respond, even in places and ways which do not now seem clear. Support one another in love, confident that my Spirit will be with you even as I have gone before you and shown you the way.*

**John 1:11-13 Power to Become**

*He came to what was his own, and his own people did not accept him. But to all who received him, who believed on his name, he gave power to become the children of God.*

**MEDITATION: Spirit Is Power**

Since spiritual experience is a reality in everyone, as solid as the experience of being loved, or the experience of the air one breathes, we should not shy away from the word Spirit. We should become fully aware of the spiritual presence around us and in us even if we realize how limited our experience of "God present to our spirit" is. For this is what divine Spirit means: God present to our spirit. Spirit is not a mysterious substance. It is not a part of God; it is God himself; but not God as Creative Ground of all things and not God as directing history and manifesting himself in its center, but God as present in communities and personalities, grasping them, inspiring them, transforming them. For Spirit is power, not natural power, but the power which drives the human spirit above itself toward what it cannot attain by itself: the love which is greater than all other gifts, the truth in which the depth of being opens itself to us, the holy which is the manifestation of the presence of the ultimate.

Paul Tillich, "Spiritual Presence," from a sermon preached in Rockefeller Chapel, Chicago, on Sunday, January 15, 1961

**Testimony of Two Apostolic Witnesses**

**The Words of Alma:**

*And thus we see the great call of the diligence of men to labor in the vineyards of the Lord... Oh, that I were an angel, and could have the wish of my heart, that I might go forth and speak with the trump of God, with a voice to shake the earth and cry repentance to every people ...But, behold, I am a man and do sin in my wish, for I ought to be content with the things which the*

*Lord has allotted to me ...Now, seeing that I know these things, why should I desire more than to perform the work to which I have been called?*

*I know that which the Lord has commanded me, and I glory in it. I do not glory in myself, but I glory in that which the Lord has commanded me. And this is my glory, that perhaps I may be an instrument in the hands of God to bring some soul to repentance and this is my joy ...And the same God has called me by a holy calling to preach the gospel to this people, and has given me much success in which my joy is full but I do not joy in my own success alone, but my joy is fuller because of the success of my brethren who have been up to the land of Nephi. Behold, they have labored exceedingly and have brought forth much fruit...*

*And now may God grant these my brethren that they may sit down in the kingdom of God, and also all those who are the fruit of their labors that they may go out no more but that they may praise him forever. Amen.*

Book of Mormon, Alma 15, selections from verses 51-69

**The Words of Paul:**

*When I came to you, brothers and sisters, I did not come proclaiming the mystery of God to you in lofty words or wisdom. For I decided to know nothing among you except Jesus Christ and him crucified. And I came to you in weakness and fear and in much trembling. My speech and my proclamation were not with plausible words of wisdom, but with a demonstration of Spirit and power, so that your faith might rest not on human wisdom but on the power of God* (1 Corinthians 2:15).

Holy Spirit, come with power; Breathe into our aching night.
We expect you this glad hour, Waiting for your strength and light.
We are joyful, we are eager, Yearning for your gracious deed;
Rest upon your congregation; Give us power of God we plead.

Holy Spirit, come with fire, Burn us with your presence new.
Let us as one mighty choir Sing our hymn of praise to you.
Burn away our wasted sadness And enflame us with your love;
Burst upon our congregation, Give us gladness from above.

Holy Spirit, bring your message; Burn and breathe each word anew
Deep into our tired living Till we strive your work to do.
Teach us love and trusting kindness; Bear our arms to those who hurt;
Breathe upon our congregation And inspire us with your Word.

Ann Neufeld Rupp, *Hymns of the Saints,* No. 287

**PRAYER:** Many are the times, O God, that you have showered your blessings upon us. Where we were weak, we became strong; where we were hesitant, we moved forward in assurance; where we were unheeding, you filled our hearts with love. Whatever the circumstance we are called to meet, may we never falter in our trust that you are there walking the path with us. It is only through your power that we can rise above ourselves to truly become your children.. With joy we accept your invitation to become one with you. Amen.

# THE THIRD THURSDAY OF EASTER: THE SPIRIT OF GUIDANCE AND DISCERNMENT

**Invocation:**

Open my eyes, O Lord, That I may see
Whatever glimpse of truth Thou hast for me.
Without thy guiding help, I shall not see.
Open my eyes, O Lord, Illumine me.

(Roy A. Cheville, *Hymns of the Saints,* No. 454.)

**SCRIPTURE:** **Psalm 31:2-5. Lead Me and Guide Me**

*You are indeed my rock and my fortress; for your name's sake lead me and guide me, take me out of the net that is hidden for me, for you are my refuge. Into your hand I commit my spirit; you have redeemed me, O Lord, faithful God.*

**Doctrine and Covenants 153:9c Trust in God's Guidance**

*Be steadfast and trust in the instructions which have been given for your guidance. I will be with you and strengthen you for the tasks that lie ahead if you will continue to be faithful and commit yourselves without reservation to the building of my kingdom.*

**Doctrine and Covenants 162:2c Discernment**

*As a prophetic people you are called under the direction of the spiritual authorities and with the common consent of the people, to discern the divine will for your own time and in the places where you serve. You live in a world with new challenges, and the world will require new forms of ministry. The priesthood must especially respond to that challenge, and the church is admonished to prayerfully consider how calling and giftedness in the Community of Christ can best be expressed in a new time.*

**MEDITATION: A Personal Experience of Guidance**

In my evangelist's blessing given to me when I was fifteen years old these words appear: "We say to you if you will be prayerful and seek the Lord's face continually, nomatter how large the problem, or how small, if you ask for his direction for that experience, there shall come to you daily from the Lord the blessings that you need and he will hear your prayers and answer them. And when you come to places in life that are difficult, and you know not which way to turn, if you will go to him, he will make it so plain that you will see your way clearly. You can be assured that he will guide you, for his angels will be with you continually, and step by step they will lead you in the way the Lord would have you go."

What a promise! I have not taken it lightly and I have recognized that the guidance promised was truly present only when I was prepared to receive. Promises were also made of doors that would open before me if I prepared myself to enter. I learned that the choices I made were important to the One who had promised to guide me but they did not limit me to only one way. Depending on how I used the opportunities before me I learned that the blessing God can create through us is possible in a variety of ways if we enter in faith and trust in the guidance promised. Seeing my way "clearly" did not always happen before choices were made. The Spirit gave me freedom to choose, but having chosen I was supported, encouraged and led on the way. That way did not eliminate dark times, in fact sometimes guided me into them, but the Spirit that was the Light of my life was a Spirit the darkness could not overcome. Both the message that came to me and the principles I learned from it are not limited to me or to any one person. They belong to us all and are there for our discovery.

Velma Ruch

### The Gift of Discernment

A basic element in guidance is the gift of discernment, the ability to discern between that which is right and that which is wrong; that which is of God and that which is not. In his book *Discerning God's Will,* Ben Campbell Johnson says that our hunger for meaning is a disguised hunger for the will of God, "a reality that has been made visible in Jesus Christ. Christ stands as the norm for discerning God's will." He goes on to speak of individual guidance and the importance of our having been created in the image of God. He then mentions the various ways in which this guidance may come to us: through intuition, imagination, memory, action. Having dealt at length with individual discernment of the will of God, he turns to corporate discernment. "In this discerning community," he writes, "we discover the will of God both for our own lives and for our mission to the world. I set forth a vision of the church as a community of discernment." He raises the question, "What faculties for discernment are accessible to the corporate community? Can we claim that those aspects of discernment available to individuals exist in the community in a corporate form? These corporate faculties include the core desire within the church, the corporate intuition, imagination, historical memory, and the risk of doing the will of God."

The answer to Johnson's question--"Can we claim that those aspects of discernment available to individuals exist in the community in a corporate form?"—is YES! In the recent past the Community of Christ has been involved with two crucial issues, both of which required the corporate discernment involving the whole body. One involved a change in the name of the church from The Reorganized Church of Jesus Christ of Latter Day Saints to Community of Christ. The second, following the resignation of President Grant McMurray, called us as a body open to the guidance of the Spirit, to discern whom God was calling to fill this demanding position. What happened in both instances, but particularly in the second, was truly amazing. We have long liked to speak of ourselves as a prophetic people. I am not sure we always knew exactly what that meant. Now we have a glimpse of how God's Spirit can disperse itself all over the world, touching people of different races and cultures, out of which grew a common testimony of God's will for us at this time. In our recent experience in the choice of a president/prophet it seems as if the testimonies and witness of all these people descended as a pillar of light on the Leadership Council as they unanimously arrived at the same name.

Richard Foster in his chapter "Guidance" in *Celebration of Discipline* refers to how the early church handled the issue of circumcision.. After the Spirit had individually touched a great variety of people, Peter, Paul, and Barnabus among them, they came together to explore this most contentious issue. The Spirit moved among them as they heard the testimonies of the servants of God. They unanimously decided on a procedure and sent Paul and Barnabus out with the news because "*it has seemed good to the Holy Spirit and to us to impose on you no further burden*" (Acts 15:28). Foster writes, "It was more than a victory regarding an issue; it was a victory of the method used in resolving all issues. As a people they had decided to live under the direct rulership of the Spirit. They had rejected both human totalitarianism and anarchy. They had even rejected democracy, that is, majority rule. They had dared to live on the basis of Spirit-rule; no fifty-one percent vote, no compromises, but Spirit-directed unity. And it worked" (178-179). The question raised by many is whether such unanimity under the impulse of the Spirit is possible today. Our answer in June 2005 is "Yes." The Spirit is as powerful today as it was in the first century if we are willing to follow its leading.

What have been you experiences in seeking the guidance of God in your life? In what ways do you believe it is possible for us to discern the will of God? Have you, perhaps in your home congregation, engaged in a process to discern the will of God? How is it possible to distinguish the word of God from all the other voices calling to you?

**PRAYER:** God of Wisdom and of Light, we seek your face continually as we walk the precarious paths of our lives. We wish to follow what you desire for us but we are often lured away by the enticing invitations from a world that does not recognize you. Help us to truly know you so we can distinguish your voice from all the other voices that call to us. We pray not only for ourselves but also for the groups of which we are a part that together we may create the kingdom of God among us. Amen.

# THE THIRD FRIDAY OF EASTER: GROWING IN THE SPIRIT

**Ask and You Shall Receive:**
**If any of you is lacking in wisdom, ask God, who gives to all generously and ungrudgingly, and it will be given you. But ask in faith, never doubting, for the one who doubts is like a wave of the sea, driven and tossed by the wind**
*(James 1:5).*

**SCRIPTURE:** **Doctrine and Covenants 159:8**

*Then, as you gain ever more confidence in sensing the leadings of my Spirit, you will begin to see with new eyes, embrace the truths that are waiting for your understanding and move joyfully toward the fulfillment of the tasks that are yours to accomplish.*

**John 16:12-13. Growing to Receive**

*I still have many things to say to you, but you cannot bear them now. When the Spirit of truth comes, he will guide you into all the truth; for he will not speak on his own, but will speak whatever he hears, and he will declare to you the things that are to come.*

**MEDITATION: Characteristics of Spirit Presence**

Of the many characteristics of Spirit presence we could consider, I will mention five: intimacy, righteousness, power, mission, and witness. These correspond to five of the movements of the spiritual life identified by Richard Foster and others as the contemplative life, the virtuous life, the charismatic life, social justice, and the evangelical life (*Devotional Classics,* Richard J. Foster and James Bryan Smith, eds. [HarperSanFrancisco, 1993], 3). Though we are likely to be drawn to one or two of these more than the others, all are necessary for balance in our spiritual lives and should find expression in the spiritual disciplines in which we engage. All of them grow out of the life of Christ. It is through Christ that we learn the ways of the Spirit with us.

**INTIMACY**

One distinguishing mark of Christ's relationship with the Father was an ever-deepening intimacy. He did not leave that intimacy to chance. Over and over again he went up into the hills to pray and often spent whole nights in meditation and prayer. But so near was the Father in him that even in the midst of crowds and personal suffering that center was the source of redemptive ministry. If that were necessary for Christ, how much more so must it be for us. Learning to live daily in intimacy with the Divine – practicing the presence, as it has been called – is an important part of our spiritual growth.

Intimacy and absence are closely entwined, each necessary to the other. The psalmist states, *"For me it is good to be near God; I have made the Lord God my refuge"* (Psalm 73:28) but the psalmist could also exclaim, "*My God, my God, why have you forsaken me?"* (Psalm 22) as did Christ on the cross. The darkness that descends upon each of us at various times in our lives is an opening for the God "*whose power is made perfect through weakness"* (2 Corinthians 12:9). Such suffering has a possibility of transforming our lives. The "ministry" of the Spirit at such a time may for awhile intensify the suffering. We do not wish it; we try to avoid it;

it is suffering devoid of joy. It is a crisis of faith where we either recognize the source of our strength or succumb to mediocrity and despair.

Such experiences, also known as "the dark night of the soul," are likely to be most severe for the spiritually adept and at important transition points in their growth. Ezekiel hid in a cave; the disciples after the crucifixion of Christ locked themselves in a room *"for fear of the Jews"*; the disciples from Emmaus were running back to a home that no longer had any meaning – that is until they met Christ. That became the transforming moment in the midst of surrounding darkness. The spirit is there, as it always is, unseen but present, stripping away the extraneous baggage of our lives and giving us the possibility of rising to new heights of being.

## RIGHTEOUSNESS

A second characteristic of spirit presence is righteousness. Christ cares about our behavior. "*I have come that you might have life and have it more abundantly,*" he said (John 10:10). Paul said that such righteousness, or fullness of being, was the result of being first rooted and grounded in love. This is the rootage that makes possible the growth of the plant of righteousness. I know of no surer test of the Spirit in our lives than the presence of this love that makes us painfully aware of our inadequacies but accepted nonetheless. As the hymn "Beneath the Cross of Jesus" states it,

> And from my stricken eyes with tears
> Two wonders I confess
> The wonder of redeeming love
> And my unworthiness.

Our response to such a touch of the Spirit is to accept with gratefulness this forgiving love but also to engage in the personal disciplines that will rid our lives of those debilitating actions which rob us of the fruits of the Spirit: "*love, joy, peace, patience, kindness, goodness, faithfulness, gentleness, self-control*" (Galatians 5:22-23).

## POWER

The power of which we speak is the power that Christ promised his disciples would be theirs. "*You shall receive power when the Holy Spirit has come upon you,*" he said (Acts 1:8). They learned what he meant on the day of Pentecost when ordinary words burst forth penetrating the minds and hearts of people from many nations, causing them to repent and turn to the Lord. Under that power barriers of social status, of sex, and of background were removed. All were called to be a prophetic people. It is under the power of the Spirit that we learn what that means for our individual lives.

"*You did not choose me but I chose you,*" said Christ (John 15:16). When we discover the miracle of being so chosen, our lives are transformed. We recognize that we are upheld and supported by a power beyond ourselves to whom we are responsible. With this recognition comes the call to an eternal vocation, a vocation that involves the totality of our lives. Our awareness of God's will for our lives is a process and is closely related to a growing sensitivity to the Spirit. A daily living in the presence of the Divine and referring all things to that Spirit will develop in us the discernment that allows us to distinguish the voice of God from all other voices that are calling to us. The voice is often very fine and subtle but nothing is more sure. All ministry is dependent on our hearing of that voice both for ourselves and for the institutions of which we are a part. We can be assured that we will be blessed by the Spirit's power as we move out in response. Spiritual gifts were given for exactly that purpose.

**MISSION AND WITNESS**

Mission and witness lead us to the corporate expression of the Spirit. Use of the Spirit just for individual satisfaction and inner peace is a betrayal of its intended function. The call of the Spirit is to community. We are called to be a people, a bonded, caring community, what has been called "a social creation of grace." The Spirit thus working among us can free us from doctrinal blinders, from willful self-interest, from deafness and near-sightedness. Our vision becomes immensely improved and we are enabled to see with new eyes the truths that were always waiting for our comprehension. It is in community, I believe, that many of those truths will emerge. It is there we lend out our minds to one another. It is there we come to a recognition of needs both expressed and unexpressed. It is there our vision becomes widened to take in those far and near in need of justice, peace, and love. It is there the Spirit works among us.

> Dietrich Bonhoeffer in writing of the cost of discipleship said discipleship was indeed costly but the cost was much less than the spiritual achievement was worth. . "Non-discipleship," Dallas Willard wrote, "costs abiding peace, a life penetrated throughout by love, faith that sees everything in the light of God's overriding governance for good, hopefulness that stands firm in the most discouraging of circumstances, power to do what is right and withstand the forces of evil. In short, it costs exactly that abundance of life Jesus said he came to bring" (*The Spirit of the Disciplines,* HarperSanFrancisco, 1991).

Adapted from Velma Ruch, "Sensing the Leading of My Spirit,"
The Aaronic Priesthood Temple Event, Independence,
Missouri, June 30, 1995

**PRAYER:** Eternal God, you who chose us from the beginning of time to be your sons and daughters, we bow before you in gratitude and love. Though we have wandered away from time to time, we have through your grace found our way back. We know our only home is in you. You created us for the joy of the abundant life and with all our hearts we wish to live in such a way that we can joyfully take our place in the communion of saints, we pray. Amen.

# THE THIRD SATURDAY OF EASTER: SPIRITUAL AUTHORITY

**Spiritual Awakening:**

*We can describe a process of spiritual awakening, but we cannot dissolve the mystery. Seeing with the eyes of the heart and feeling the transformation that follows create a new perspective on life, but none can fully explain how or why it happens*

(Ben Campbell Johnson, *Living Before God*).

**SCRIPTURE:** **Matthew 7:21-29 The People Were Astounded.**

*Now when Jesus had finished saying these things, the crowds were astounded at his teaching, for he taught them as one having authority and not as their scribes.*

**MEDITATION: Spiritual Authority**

We might ask, by what authority do the children of God speak to the world? The question of authority is a difficult one with many complexities, but I am not now concerned with official authority but rather with spiritual authority, the authority of the lives of those who confess the Lord. Our lives must always give authenticity to the message. Remember again the powerful words of President Grant McMurray's call to transformation at World Conference in 1996:

Hear me now! We will *become* ... Not we will believe. Not we will affirm. Not we will espouse or proclaim or embrace or declare or try to be. We will *become!*

But how do we become such people? It all begins with our heart's desire that leads to an encounter with Christ. The encounter alerts us to the call which gives us courage to say yes. This initiates a life of prayer and worship, which makes possible growth in discipleship and dedication to spiritual servanthood. It is the work of a lifetime but as Evelyn Underhill said to some Anglican priests in 1926, it is "part of the apostolic process of sanctifying yourselves for the sake of other souls." It means that we become what we proclaim.

I was much interested in the story written by Douglas Steere about Thomas Kelly. From his youth on Thomas Kelly was a deeply committed person. He felt a call and had a sense of mission. In the process he experienced the discouragement, even despair, of those who had caught a great vision and sensed that others did not feel the same urgency and were not willing to pay the price. Then something happened. No one knows exactly what it was but the part of him that was divided grew together and became whole. The change in him became evident in three lectures he gave at a Germantown Friends Meeting in January 1938. Douglas Steere writes:

> At Germantown, people were deeply moved and said, "This is authentic." His writings and spoken messages began to be marked by a note of experiential authority ...It was the same voice, the same pen, the same rich imagery that always crowded his writing, and on the whole a remarkably similar set of religious ideas. But now he seemed to be expounding less as one possessed of "knowledge about" and more as one who had had "unmistakable acquaintance with."
>
> Thomas Kelley, *A Testament of Devotion* (SanFrancisco: Harper and Row, 1941)

> That "unmistakable acquaintance with" will always be the mark of those who have experienced Christ firsthand and who carry his presence in their lives. They know what it means to sense the leadings of the Spirit and in their growing competency and understanding move joyfully toward the fulfillment of the tasks that are theirs to accomplish (D. and C. 159:8). There is a power that is part of our inheritance as followers of Christ. We need to expect it and trust it and move out in confidence that we will be so sustained.
>
> Velma Ruch, *The Transforming Power of Prayer,* Vol. 2, 186-187

What does spiritual authority mean to you? Think of two or three people you believe carry that authority. How is it manifested? The spirit of discernment is necessary to distinguish between a pretense to such authority and the real thing. What tests do you personally apply to tell the difference?

Do you recognize in your own life when you have that presence, that authority? Even if no one tells you, how do you know? Can you think of experiences in your own life when you moved from "knowledge about" to "acquaintance with"?

**PRAYER:** Transforming God in whom we live and move and have our being, you have held us so tenderly, loved us so completely, and ever guided us by your wisdom. Because we belong to you and have been touched by your Spirit we wish to carry that Spirit with us always. May there be nothing in our lives that will hinder the flow of your Spirit through us to others. Wherever we are we wish to be your representatives to a world in need. In the name of the living Christ, we pray. Amen.

# THE FOURTH WEEK OF EASTER
## THEME: I AM ...

## THE FOURTH SUNDAY OF EASTER: WHO IS GOD?

O love of God, how strong and true,
Eternal and yet ever new;
Uncomprehended and unbought,
Beyond all knowledge and all thought.

Horatio Bonar, *Hymns of the Saints,* No. 188.

**SCRIPTURE:** **Exodus 3:13-15 "What Is His Name?"**

*But Moses said to God, "If I come to the Israelites and say to them, 'The God of your ancestors has sent me to you' and they ask me, 'What is his name?' what shall I say to them?" God said to Moses, "I Am who I Am. This is my name forever, and this my title for all generations."*

**MEDITATION: "I Am Who I Am"**

*God said to Moses, "I Am who I Am"* Part of the richness of the Bible is the variety of names it uses to address and speak of God. This story describes how Israel came to know the unique and most cherished name it had for God – Yahweh, Jehovah, or the Lord. Though the name occurs earlier in the biblical text, here it is both given to Moses and Israel for the first time and connected to the "God of your ancestors," whose presence and faithfulness Israel already knew ...

> [One interpretation of the name] uses Yahweh as a causative verb, "He causes to be." This points to God as the One who creates and sustains the world and who acts powerfully in it with loving purpose, two powerful themes throughout the Old Testament. This is the God who is mover and shaker, the One who makes things happen ...The God who sends Moses is the God who acts. What better God to announce to Hebrew slaves who long for deliverance? What better God to rely on in our own longings?
>
> *The Renovare Spiritual Formation Bible,* Richard J. Foster, ed., 102; used with permission

**"One Atom of Myself Sustains the Universe"**

It is impossible to express the essence of God in terms of himself. He can be understood only in terms of other things. In the Hindu *Bhagavad-Gita* when the disciple Arjuna asks the divine Krishna to reveal who he really is, the light of his innermost nature, Krishna replies:

> *O Arjuna, I am the divine seed of all lives. In this world nothing animate or inanimate exists without me . . . Whatever in this world is powerful, beautiful or glorious that you may know to have come forth from a fraction of my power and glory.*
>
> *But what need have you Arjuna, to know this huge variety? Know only that I exist and that one atom of myself sustains the universe.*
>
> *Bhagavad-Gita: The Song of God,* trans. Swami Prabhavananda and Christopher Isherwood (New York: Mentor Religious Classics, 1951), 89-90

Beautiful and inspiring as these descriptions are, we know that they only partially reveal the truth about Krishna; nevertheless, the comparisons with human experience open the doors of our understanding to the greater light. John Milton dealt with this means of knowing in his exposition on Christian doctrine:

> Our safest way is to form in our minds such a conception of God, as shall correspond with his own delineation and representation of himself in the sacred writings. For granting that both in the literal and figurative description of God, he is exhibited not as he really is, but in such a manner as may be within the scope of our comprehensions yet yet we ought to entertain such a conception of him, as he, in condescending to accommodate himself to our capacities, has shown that he desires we should conceive. For it is on this very account that he has lowered himself to our level, let in our flights above the reach of human understanding, and beyond the written word of Scripture, we should be tempted to indulge in vague cogitations and subtleties.
>
> John Milton, *Complete Poems and Major Prose,* Merritt Y. Hughes, ed. (New York: Odyssey Press, 1957), 905

> So it is with Christ as he attempts to reveal to his followers who he really is. The Gospel of John is replete with symbols of the Divine. "*I am the bread of life"; "I am the light of the world'; "I am the gate for the sheep"; "I am the good Shepherd"; "I am the way, the truth, and the life"; "I am the vine and you are the branches."* In all of these the access to the infinite is through the finite. This approach not only reveals to us something about the Divine but adds preciousness and significance to the everyday experiences of our lives.
>
> Velma Ruch. *Signature of God,* 38-41

The "I am" statements continually force us to ask, "Is Jesus who he says he is?" Is he the Bread of my life? Do I live by his Light? Do I enter through him as the Gate to salvation, or do I keep trying to rescue myself? Do I trust him to shepherd me? Do I depend on his Resurrection , or do I keep trying to lift myself up? Do I let him be the Way for me or do I keep asking for directions? Is he the Truth by which I judge all lesser truths? Is he my Life, or do I employ entertainments to bring me life? Do I abide in him, cling to him as a branch to a Vine, and draw all my spiritual nourishment from him?

*The Renovare Spiritual Formation Bible,* 1936; used with permission

**PRAYER:** Praise to the living God! All praised be thy name
Who e'er hast been and e'er shalt be, and still the same.
The one eternal God ere aught that now appears;
The first, the last, beyond all thought through timeless years.

Eternal life hast thou implanted in the soul;
Thy love shall be our strength and stay while ages roll
Praise to the living God, all praised be thy name
Who e'er hast been and e'er shalt be, and still the same.
Based on the Yigdal of Daniel Ben Judah,
*Hymns of the Saints,* No. 47

# THE FOURTH MONDAY OF EASTER: I AM THE BREAD OF LIFE

**Invocation:**

Break thou the bread of life, Dear Lord, to me,
As thou didst break the loaves beside the sea;
Beyond the sacred page, I seek thee, Lord;
My spirit pants for thee, O living Word.

Mary A. Lathbury, *Hymns of the Saints,* No. 173

**SCRIPTURE:** **John 6:25-40; 48-51 Nourishment through Christ**

*Jesus said to them, "I am the bread of life. Whoever comes to me will never be hungry, and whoever believes in me will never be thirsty."*

**MEDITATION: Manna Sent from God**

The two staples of life are bread and water. Jesus is saying he is both of those. He is like the manna sent from God to sustain life, to bless. But it is eternal life of which he speaks and spiritual life he is to sustain for all who believe in Him. Jesus, just prior to the quoted scripture has been feeding the five thousand, walking on water, healing the paralyzed man by the pool, healing an official's son, and has met with the Samaritan woman at the well. Yet the followers ask for another sign, another proof that he is who he says he is. He tells them they must work for the living bread and the work is faith. The followers' response finally is, "Sir, give us this bread always." I wonder if they understood what they were asking, if they truly knew the work required.

Those of you who bake bread, no matter what type, know of the details which are necessary to get the desired results. The particular recipe I most often use is a sourdough recipe. I first have to take the starter out of the refrigerator and "feed" it. After the starter sits for several hours so the yeast is activated, I can then begin to mix the dough. The flour must be carefully measured and sometimes sifted to remove lumps. The remainder of the ingredients are added, then the thick dough must be stirred, mixed, and kneaded carefully and completely to get the desired consistency. I have done it enough times now to do it by the way the dough feels and the way it pulls away from my fingers rather than depend entirely on the measurements. Then there is the period of waiting for the dough to rise. When it is at a proper level of expansion, the dough is pressed down, divided into chunks and kneaded before forming the loaves which are placed into pans to again rise before baking. The process is not one that can be hurried and sometimes I have to wait longer than others for the dough to get to the right height in the pans before baking. When the loaves are placed in the oven, I must be careful to put them in the right place in the oven and not touching each other and for the right amount of time and temperature to get the type of loaves I want. If anyone is present when the loaves come out of the oven or if someone comes in shortly thereafter, the desire is always to have some of the fresh baked bread while it is still warm. Unless I have promised all of the loaves to others beforehand, the answer is always yes. I serve the warm, soft, crust covered slices with butter if desired but seldom with anything else. There is satisfaction, pleasure and joy in the process and in the sharing.

While this is a process for physical bread, there are many parallels for the bread of which Jesus spoke. Were the disciples ready for the bread? In asking for the Bread of Life did they realize they must, too, become bread?

> Were they ready to be sifted, to have the less desirable parts of their lives shaken away, removed, changed? Were they ready to have the "lumps" removed? The lumps of pride, selfishness and judgmental attitudes? Were they ready to be refined and purified so that only pure kernel, ground to a fine usable texture was left? Were they ready to receive the added ingredients; the leaven, salt, oil and water that would transform them into new creatures? Were they ready to be kneaded; pushed, pulled, stretched and formed into different shapes than they had ever known? Were they ready for the Holy fire that would burn away all impurities and make them useful to be consumed in their work of proclaiming Christ? Did they realize this work could not be hurried, that it would require a lifetime? I doubt they completely understood if they had any idea at all.
> Edith Gallaher, Sermon preached in Lamoni, Iowa, August 6, 2000

What does Jesus' description of himself as "the bread of life" mean to you? If you accept that description do you see its relation to your own life? What transformation must occur in you before you can truly be the bread of life for another?

**PRAYER:** Jesus, Bread blessed and broken, you ask me to be your leaven. You lift me to your Father and gift me with your loving.

I, just a handful of dough, am asked to be the leaven for a whole batch of people so that faith will rise in hearts. It is humbling to be your leaven. It is risky to be your holy. It is goodness to be your dough.

I, just a handful of dough, am called by you to be kneaded, to bear the imprints of trust, giving life shaped by daily dyings.

I, just a handful of dough, know so little about being leaven. Yet, you lift me up repeatedly, telling me that you love me, assuring me with the truth that you are my rising strength. Jesus, first one blessed and broken, make of me a good handful of dough, one who trusts enough to be kneaded, one who loves enough to be shared. Amen.

Joyce Rupp, *Fresh Bread* (Notre Dame, Indiana: Ave Maria Press, 1985)

# THE FOURTH TUESDAY OF EASTER: I AM THE LIGHT OF THE WORLD

**Invocation:**

Holy and creative Light, We invoke thy kindling ray;
Dawn upon our spirits' night; Turn our darkness into day.
Work in all, in all renew Day by day the life divine;
All our wills to thee subdue; All our hearts to thee incline. Amen.
Frederick Henry Hedge, *Hymns of the Saints,* No. 12

**SCRIPTURE:** **John 8:12-20; 9:5 The Light of Life**

*Again Jesus spoke to them, saying, "I am the light of the world. Whoever follows me will not walk in darkness but will have the light of life." "As long as I am in the world, I am the light of the world."*

**MEDITATION: The Light of Christ Within**

The Inner Light, the Inward Christ, is no mere doctrine, belonging peculiarly to a small religious fellowship, to be accepted or rejected as a mere belief. It is the living Center of Reference for all Christian souls and Christian groups – yes, and of non-Christian groups as well – who seriously mean to dwell in the secret place of the Most High. He is the center and source of action, not the end-point of thought. He is the locus of commitment, not a problem for debate. Practice comes first in religion, not theory or dogma. And Christian practice is not exhausted in outward deeds. These are the fruits, not the roots.

Thomas Kelly, *A Testament of Devotion*
(San Francisco: Harper and Row, 1941), 34-35; used with permission

**Where the Light Leads**

There always will be elements of the unknown as that holy and creative light floods our being. Joseph Smith did not know what would be the result of that short walk to the grove to pray. Neither did Isaiah when in his blazing moment he stammered forth the words, "Here am I; send me." Neither did Mary when she agreed to bear the child that would become Savior of the world. The creative light will always put us at risk. It catapults us to the frontier and it is always unknown out there. The paths are not clearly marked. We are called to explore. It is possible to veer from the central light ever so slightly and find that that small turning led into other turnings until like Dante we wake up and find ourselves lost in a dark wood. But we have helpers – the Spirit of God, our own integrity, and the corrective influence of one another. Moreover, we need the gift of what the ancient writers called "discernment of spirits." We need to be able to distinguish the "Light of the world" from the many flashing lights that surround us daily. Once having truly experienced that Light we have a measuring rod by which we can test all the other "lights" that surround us.

**Light Growing Out of Darkness**

Once in the nineties I took a tour group to the North Cape to see the midnight sun. It was June 15 but when we arrived on the island where the North Cape is located it was snowing hard. If we were to see the midnight sun we had to travel 22 miles up ice-covered mountain roads only navigable by busses with chains. On that particular night the journey seemed a fools' errand. No sun could be seen through the snow and the clouds, but we decided to make the journey anyway. Once up there, all was stark and cold. We stood on the edge of the mountain and looked out over the Arctic Sea. It seemed like the end of the world. We went inside the guest house to comfort ourselves with some hot chocolate. Suddenly some one shouted, "The clouds are parting." We all ran out. It was almost midnight and there in all its glory was the midnight sun! How wondrous it seemed and how unexpected. Without the previous ice and darkness, the sun would not have seemed nearly so glorious.

Sometimes we miss the light because we are not willing to risk the journey. That risk is sometimes substantial and without proper preparation can be foolhardy. It took busses with chains to get up the mountain. Where do we get the chains or the nourishment necessary for the journey? Certainly, the sacraments are a primary means as are the many spiritual disciplines that help us grow in light and truth. For us the challenge to risk the journey was available to us for only a few minutes. Procrastination or further preparation was not an option. Either we went then or that door was closed to us and the glory of the midnight sun would exist only in our dreams. So important are the seemingly unrelated decisions we make each day. Crisis is always.

**PRAYER:**

Lord, lead me by your Spirit into a better light,
In truth and understanding and knowledge of your will
I confess my sin before you, confess my lack of love.
Will you bring to life my vision, my sense of awe, my faith.

You're ever true and faithful in meeting all my need.
I barely comprehend you; I often am afraid.
Enable me to seek you with all my heart and mind,
And to find the reassurance in the mystery you are.

In endless care and presence, you give to every life
Compassion overflowing and love that's deep and wise.
Grant that I in glad responding may surely find the strength
To share the Christ with others, loving freely, bearing grace.

Eric L. Selden *Hymns of the Saints,* No. 183

# THE FOURTH WEDNESDAY OF EASTER: I AM THE DOOR OF THE SHEEPFOLD

**Admonition:**

*"Strive to enter through the narrow door; for many, I tell you, will try to enter and will not be able"*
*(Luke 13:24).*

**SCRIPTURE:** **John 10:7 – 10 IV Entering the Door**

*Then said Jesus unto them again, "Verily, verily, I say unto you, I am the door of the sheepfold...I am the door; by me if any man enter in, he shall be saved, and shall go in and out and find pasture...I am come that they might have life and have it more abundantly."*

**MEDITATION: The Door**

The door is one of our most powerful images. What exists on one side of the door is different from what we discover on the other side. The open door may be an invitation in to the warmth of hospitality, to opportunity, to new life; or it may open to certain problems, sorrows and difficulties that will challenge us to the roots of our very being. The door that closes against us is also significant. The dilemma we face is how hard we should knock to make the door open for us. That decision needs all the guidance and wisdom the Spirit can bestow on us. Doors of prejudice, of hatred, of unconcern are doors that need to be opened so the light of love can be let in. Doors that stand in the way of our personal desires and progress may need a careful reassessment of what we think we want. The closed door may be there for a purpose to cause us to realign our goals but it may be there to test our resolve in carrying out the work to which we have been called. Doors open or closed can determine who we become.

Jesus entered the door of our humanity as a little child lying in a manger. But despite the song of the angels and the star in the East, as John tells us, "*He came unto his own and his own received him not.*" The one by whom the worlds were created and from whom we have our very being came to his rightful domain and was rejected. No doors opened to receive him. He was despised and afflicted, a man of sorrows and acquainted with grief. "In Jesus Christ," John Mogabgab has written, "God has tasted to the full the precarious existence of a stranger in an unfamiliar land. But the excluded God is in reality the inclusive host who invites to the banquet not only the privileged and well respected, but also the destitute and disparaged."

The marvel for us is that the One who came to his own and found the door shut against him is the one who offered to all the open door of healing and abundant life. There was the woman taken in adultery to whom he spoke those words of grace, "*Neither do I condemn thee, go and sin no more.*" There was Zaccheus, the tax collector, perched in his sycamore tree, "*Come down, Zaccheus, for today I must abide with you in your house.*" There were those fishermen busy along the shores of Lake Galilee to whom he said, "*Come, follow me, and I will make you fishers of men.*" There was the blind man, Bartimeus, to whom he said, *"What do you want?" "Lord, I want to see."* And he was granted his sight. To the woman at the well he said, "*Those who drink of the water I give will never thirst again.*"

The One who was rejected and despised by the majority gave to all who received him the power to become the children of God. Anyone who is blessed by entering the open door offered by Christ is privileged to become an open door of blessing for others. It is an axiom that when we are blessed, we bless. Because God gives us love, we have love to give. We play these roles simultaneously. Unless we receive we cannot give and unless we give, the thirst-quenching power of living water dries up in us.

How did you enter in to the door Jesus opened for you? How did you become a disciple? What doors have you opened for others? Have you experienced closed doors in your life? Did you discover later that some of them were closed so that other more profitable doors would open for you? Are there some doors you are still knocking on that need to open when you are ready? While you are knocking are you also aware that Jesus is knocking on your door? Are you willing to open to let him in?

**PRAYER:** Dear Inviting Savior, you who opened the door to my greatest joy, I thank you. In walking through the door of baptism I consecrated myself to follow you wherever that journey might lead. Forgive me for the lapses in my commitment and help me to rise with you in newness of life. May I not be deaf to your gentle knock on the door of my heart and may my response include all those to whom I am called to minister. Amen.

# THE FOURTH THURSDAY OF EASTER: I AM THE GOOD SHEPHERD

**The Promise:**

*He will feed his flock like a shepherd; he will gather his lambs in his arms, and carry them in his bosom, and gently lead the mother sheep (Isaiah 40:11).*

**SCRIPTURE:** **John 10:11-18 The Good Shepherd Cares**

*"I am the good shepherd. The good shepherd lays down his life for the sheep."*

**Luke 15:1-7. The Lost Is Found**

*"Which one of you having a hundred sheep and losing one of them, does not leave the ninety-nine in the wilderness and go after the one that is lost until he finds it? When he has found it, he lays it on his shoulder and rejoices. And when he comes home, he calls together his friends and neighbors, saying to them, 'Rejoice with me, for I have found my sheep that was lost.' Just so, I tell you, there will be more joy in heaven over one sinner who repents than over ninety-nine righteous persons who need no repentance.*

**Psalm 23 The Lord Is My Shepherd**

*The Lord is my shepherd, I shall not want.*
*He makes me lie down in green pastures;*
*he leads me beside still waters;*
*he restores my soul.*
*He leads me in right paths for his name's sake.*
*Even though I walk through the darkest valley,*
*I fear no evil; for you are with me;*
*your rod and your staff– they comfort me.*
*You prepare a table before me*
*in the presence of my enemies;*
*you anoint my head with oil; my cup overflows.*
*Surely goodness and mercy shall follow me*
*all the days of my life,*
*and I shall dwell in the house of the Lord*
*my whole life long.*

**MEDITATION: The Image of the Good Shepherd**

Jesus as the Good Shepherd , this sheltering image of the Divine, is related to a foundational desire in each of us to experience the trustworthy and sustaining ground of love out of which we come and back to which we all proceed. About this image, Wendy Wright has written:

> The depiction of Jesus as good shepherd is an ancient one in the church. Wall paintings in the catacombs at Rome show us as much. The image has not lost its communicative power through time even though the actual referent – the shepherd—is not a familiar feature of our present culture. In Jesus' own day, when shepherding was a common occupation

with which people were acquainted, the referent was clearer. Everyone knew exactly how diligently the conscientious shepherd had to work, how much he guarded against losing a lamb to straying or marauding animals. A shepherd and his flock were inseparable. The sheep were guided to lush grazing fields and fresh water by their shepherd's solicitous care.

Even today the image holds power, and we are moved by it. Perhaps it is its archetypal quality, ...that communicates to us in some nonverbal way the protective, guiding nature of the divine source. Perhaps it is not simply chance that the most popular psalm of the psalter is the twenty-third, the psalm that so many generations of children have committed to memory and that shapes so many people's image of God. The riches of this simple prayer never seem to be exhausted. The lush springtime imagery, the promise of restoration, nourishment, shelter, and blessing call up in us a deep response.

Wendy M. Wright, *The Rising (*Upper Room Books, 1994), 145-146

**The Drama of the Double Search**

Out in front of us is the drama of men and of nations, seething, struggling, laboring, dying. Upon this tragic drama in these days our eyes are all set in anxious watchfulness and in prayer. But within the silences of the souls of men an eternal drama is ever being enacted, in these days as well as in others. And on the outcome of this inner drama rests, ultimately, the outer pageant of history. It is the drama of the Hound of Heaven baying relentlessly upon the track of man. It is the drama of the lost sheep wandering in the wilderness, restless and lonely, feebly searching, while over the hills comes the wiser Shepherd. For His is a shepherd's heart, and He is restless until he holds His sheep in His arms. It is the drama of the Eternal Father drawing the prodigal home unto Himself, where there is bread enough and to spare. It is the drama of the Double Search, as Rufus Jones calls it. And always its chief actor is – the Eternal God of Love.

It is to one strand in this inner drama, one scene, where the shepherd has found His sheep, that I would direct you. It is the life of absolute and complete and holy obedience to the voice of the Shepherd. But ever throughout the account the accent will be laid upon God. God the initiator, God the aggressor, God the seeker, God the stirrer into life. God the ground of our obedience, God the giver of the power to become the children of God.

Thomas R. Kelly, *A Testament of Devotion*, 51-52; used with permission

**PRAYER:** *Now may the God of peace, who brought back from the dead our Lord Jesus, the great shepherd of the sheep, by the blood of the eternal covenant, make you complete in everything good so that you may do his will, working among us that which is pleasing in his sight, through Jesus Christ, to whom be the glory forever and ever. Amen* (Hebrews 13: 20-21).

# THE FOURTH FRIDAY OF EASTER: "I AM THE WAY, THE TRUTH AND THE LIFE"

**Invocation:**

**Make me to know your ways, O Lord; teach me your paths. Lead me in your truth, and teach me, for you are the God of my salvation; for you I wait all day long** *(Psalm 25:4-5).*

**SCRIPTURE: John 14:4-6 "How Can We Know the Way?"**

*"And you know the way to the place I am going." Thomas said to him, "Lord, we do not know where you are going. How can we know the way?" Jesus said to him, "I am the way, and the truth, and the life. No one comes to the Father except through me."*

**MEDITATION: Finding the Way**

On Bardstown Road, between Louisville and Bardstown, Kentucky, there used to be a billboard that inevitably caught my attention. It read: "Does the road you're on lead to my place? Signed God." That sign always stopped me short. In the New Testament, the same word, *hodos,* translates as both road and way. In John's Gospel, when Thomas asked Jesus, "How can we know the way?" Jesus' answer was enigmatic: "I AM the Way…" Can I ever know whether I am on the track to God? What I would really like, of course, is a personalized, prescient itinerary –just ahead is a sharp curve in the road, or a steep incline; here you will run out of gas; there you will get stuck in the mud; here you are going to crash. What *did* Jesus men when he said "I am the Way"?

Early in my life, I felt sure that if I tried very earnestly to stay close to the Jesus of the Gospels and that if I followed the laws and disciplines of my church and of religious community, I would be safe. There were many issues I did not have to think about because I had been told the answers. I had a kind of package deal that would guarantee my salvation. Looking back now, I believe I was indeed "on the way"; I was as authentically myself as it was possible for me to be at that time. The valuable formation of those early years gave me a sense of discipline and taught me humility and reverence for a trusted tradition.

Life was expanding my perceptions …The Way was obviously present in ways I had not recognized. Life was more wonderfully diverse, more fraught with complexity and mystery, than I had allowed. It required more responsibility on my part. I knew the value of church teaching and, especially of companions on the journey, but there was room for risking mistakes, maybe even some value in mistakes. My experience confirmed that there are no dead-ends; there are always new beginnings. My search for God deepened and broadened. The Way was no fixed path but was…well…on the way …

In fact, I do not believe there is A WAY in the sense of a road-map-like road ahead. The Way comes into being as, surrendering our security into the hands of the God of Jesus, we trustingly take the next step. Ordinarily we have grace enough only to see the next small step. But it is enough.

God is and has been all along at the core of our being, dwelling within us and all around us. Community and church tradition are indispensable, but we are learning to rely on that imperceptible presence and to recognize and respect with an entirely new understanding the utter mystery and incomprehensibility of God. The eyes of our hearts are opening to recognize that the whole of creation, including our own unique being is grounded in an immense love. That is Jesus' gift of the Spirit. The Way is firmly rooted in our hearts.

> There are no guarantees. There is a very steady, trusting faith—faith no longer centered in truths, but in the Truth of Life as we discover it in the Way. There is hope and trust that Paul's word might be our own life's truth; "*It is no longer I who live, but it is Christ who lives in me*" (Gal. 2:20). And always there is love. The greatest of these is love.
>
> Elaine M. Prevallet, "Finding the Way," *Weavings* (November/December 2001): 24-30

**PRAYER:** At times, O God, we are as confused as Thomas was that night in the upper room when he really had no idea what Jesus meant by saying, "*I am the way, the truth and the life.*" Thomas came to know later as we are coming to know as well. Experiencing the walk with you on our spiritual journey is teaching us so much. Because we have known your presence we recognize there is no other way that can entice us away from your way. We have no language to express to you our gratitude for the great gift of your love but we can continue to accept your invitation and to walk with you on the path to the abundant life. That is our desire. Amen.

# THE FOURTH SATURDAY OF EASTER: I AM THE VINE AND YOU ARE BRANCHES

**Spiritual Nourishment:**

Our spiritual life cannot be measured by success as the world measures it, but only by what God pours through us – and we cannot measure that at all

(Oswald Chambers, *My Utmost for His Highest*).

**SCRIPTURE:** **John 15:1-11 Abiding in the Vine**

*"I am the true vine and my Father is the vinegrower. He removes every branch in me that bears no fruit. Every branch that bears fruit he prunes to make it bear more fruit...*

*"Abide in me as I abide in you. Just as the branch cannot bear fruit by itself unless it abides in the vine, neither can you unless you abide in me. I am the vine, you are the branches. Those who abide in me and I in them bear much fruit, because apart from me you can do nothing...I have said these things to you so that my joy may be in you, and that your joy may be complete."*

**MEDITATION: Pruning of the Branches**

A vineyard is cultivated for one end alone: the maturation, harvest, and pressing of grapes. By virtue of its specialized purpose, the vineyard requires constant attention. For some vintners this may mean close monitoring of soil chemistry, while for others it may involve special concern about changing weather conditions or invading insects. Among the many activities that might be required to assure the health of a vineyard, one is required without exception: pruning. Without regular pruning, precious energy dissipates in wild, unproductive directions. The experienced vinedresser knows just how much to trim the vines so they can produce full and savory fruit.

> God desires that we be abundantly fruitful and acts to help this happen. With enduring faithfulness and intimate knowledge of our capacities, the heavenly Vinedresser provides opportunities for us to shed the excess burdens that inhibit our full maturation in God's service ... Pruning can certainly be uncomfortable. It strips us of what is non-essential to the power of God's life rising within us. But it also gathers and focuses energies previously dispersed in draining distractions or even apparently worthful commitments. Pruning concentrates the savor of the fruit we bear, for it proceeds from inward peace and promotes outward goodness. Therefore the effect of the Vinedresser's skilled hands is always a power of life greater than that which we would or could choose on our own.
>
> John S. Mogabgab, "Editor's Introduction," *Weavings* (September/October 2001): 2-3; used with permission

**Abide in Me as I Abide in You**

In Jesus' analogy of the vine, the "true vine" is not Israel or the church (a people in God, a community charged to bear much fruit): The vine is Jesus himself. His life, his love, his communion with the Father, the shedding of his blood (the fruit of the vine) create the possibility of the true people of God. We are members of the body of Christ not because of our ancestry or our own good works, but simply because we abide in him, absolutely dependent on the life he offers.

The significance of this difference is huge. It means not only that no fruitful life is possible apart from such abiding; it means that such abiding in Christ, radically available to the life he longs to pour into us, will bear fruit we could never, by ourselves, produce – or even imagine.

The heart of our vocation as Christians is not achieving ambitious goals of our own devising. Our vocation is simply to stay so indissolubly attached to Jesus, the true vine, "*that Christ may dwell in our hearts*" (see Ephesians 3:17). The essence of our call is a mystical union with Christ so deep that we, *"being rooted and grounded in love,"* may "*know the love of Christ that surpasses knowledge," that we may be filled with all the fullness of God"* (Ephesians 3:17, 19).

> Following this call will not lead us into a kind of passive quietism that is absorbed in its own mystical consolations and unconcerned with the needs of the world. Rather, surrendering to the *fullness* of God will inexorably draw us deeper into a passionate, self-giving love for the world God loves.
>
> Deborah Smith Douglas, "Vine and Branches: Abiding in Christ," *Weavings* (September/October 2001): 26.; used with permission

**Not I But Christ in Me**

> "Christ in me" means something quite different from the weight of an impossible ideal, something far more glorious than the oppression of a pattern for ever beyond all imitation. "Christ in me" means Christ bearing me along from within, Christ the motive-power that carries me on. Christ giving my whole life a wonderful poise and lift, and turning every burden into wings. All this is in it when the apostle speaks of "*Christ in you, the hope of glory"* (Colossians 1:27). Compared with this, the religion which bases everything on example is pitifully rudimentary. This, and this alone, is the true Christian religion. Call it mysticism or not – the name matters little: the thing, the experience, matters everything. To be "in Christ," to have Christ within, to realize your creed not as something you have to bear but as something by which you are borne, this is Christianity. It is more: it is release and liberty, life with an endless song at its heart. It means feeling within you, as long as life here lasts, the carrying power of Love Almighty; and underneath you, when you come to die, the touch of everlasting arms.
>
> James Stewart, *A Man in Christ* (Hodder and Stoughton), 154

**PRAYER:** O Jesus, true vine as you are, may I always receive my strength through you. You are the nourishment and motive power that carry me on. Without you, I am nothing.
May you always abide in me as I in you, I pray. Amen.

# THE FIFTH WEEK OF EASTER
# THEME: LIVING THE STORY

## THE FIFTH SUNDAY OF EASTER: LONELINESS, LONGING, SOLITUDE,HOME

**The Longing:**
**Our hearts are restless until they rest in Thee**
(Augustine, *The Confessions*).

**SCRIPTURE:** **Psalm 63:1-4 My Soul Thirsts for You**

*O God, you are my God, I seek you,*
*my soul thirsts for you;*
*my flesh faints for you,*
*as in a dry and weary land*
*where there is no water.*
*So I have looked upon you in the sanctuary,*
*beholding your power and glory.*
*Because your steadfast love is*
*better than life,*
*my lips will praise you*
*So I will bless you as long as I live;*
*I will lift up my hands and call*
*on your name.*

**Psalm 42 When Shall I Behold the Face of God?**

*As a deer longs for flowing streams*
*so my soul longs for you, O God.*
*My soul thirsts for God, for the living God.*
*When shall I come and behold the face of God?*
*My tears have been my food day and night,*
*while people say to me continually,*
*"Where is your God?"*

**MEDITATION: Loneliness and Solitude**

Richard Foster begins his chapter on solitude in *Celebration of Discipline* with the words, "Jesus calls us from loneliness to solitude" (p. 96). That is indeed so. But Jesus can use loneliness as well. How that can happen is the theme of this meditation.

Loneliness – both the good and the bad – is very much a part of the biblical record. The cry of the psalmist in Psalm 22, *"My God, my God, why have you forsaken me?"* and echoed by Jesus on the cross is a good example. The pain of being alone is expressed in Psalm 38, *"My friends and companions stand aloof from my affliction and my neighbors stand afar off."* And there are many others. A Canadian pastor, Douglas Plaskett, has said, "Loneliness is built in. Obviously it is the intention of the Creator."

He goes on to say,

> What is the purpose of loneliness? In short, it is God's way of drawing us out of ourselves, towards himself and toward our fellowman. It is his way of assuring that we keep striving to love and be loved. It is his way of assuring that we keep reaching beyond ourselves. To come back to the human community from the depression of loneliness, one must know the agony of broken communication, of unanswered doubts and questions, one must know the clear visions of loneliness and solitude – the joy of being born again.
>
> *Pulpit Digest* (July/August 1982)

We began with the statement "Jesus calls us from loneliness to solitude." Now we ask, What is solitude and how is that journey accomplished ? Foster gave one simple definition: "Loneliness is inner emptiness; solitude is inner fulfillment." The poet, Byron, spoke of the solitude where we are least alone. How can we move from one to the other? It all begins with desire, as Alma admonishes us in chapter 16 of the Book of Alma. We begin with desire and with the trust that the seed we plant will bear fruit. The possibility of living life in the presence of the Spirit is open to anyone who has the desire and is willing to let down the barriers that keep the holy out. This cannot be accomplished without solitude because solitude is very closely related to practicing the Presence. Solitude is not necessarily related to place or even being alone. Solitude is possible in the midst of noisy crowds. It is, as Foster says, inner attentiveness. It means learning how to listen to that still, small voice and to be in a place that is not a place: the presence of the living God.

**Hunger**

"All life is but a wandering to find home," sighs Murphy in Beckett's novel of the same name. Murphy is right. No theme is more persistent in literature than this journey into the unknown, this impulsion – at whatever cost – to find home. What is the something within us that drives us so? Would we strive so hard and endure so much if we were not certain, even when hope grows dim of finding? Dag Hammarskjold, who persistently sought for "that clear, pure note" of home wrote in *Markings:*

I am being driven forward
into an unknown land.
The pass grows steeper,
the air colder and sharper.
A wind from my unknown goal
stirs the strings
of expectation.

Still the question,
Shall I ever get there?
There where life resounds,
A clear pure note
In the silence. (p. 5)

Augustine in his great chapter on memory in *The Confessions* asks two crucial questions, "Why do we so diligently seek for happiness? Is it because we remember joy?"

> Is not the happy life that which all men will to have, and no man entirely wills against? Where have they known it, that they in such wise will to possess it? here have they seen it, so that they love it? ...Unless we knew it, we would not love it...Is this like the way we remember joy? Perhaps so, for even when I am sad, I remember my joys, just as when wretched I remember the happy life ... Where, then, and when did I have experience of my happy life, so that I remember it, and love it, and long for it?... although one man seeks it in one way and the other in a different way, there is one thing that they all strive to attain, that is, to have joy.
>
> pp. 248-251

Augustine concludes that we cannot long for something we do not know. From his own experience he affirms that the Divine has set his signet upon us and that "our hearts are restless" until they rest in him. When our reason, our wills, our lives are aligned with his, then, and then only, do we arrive home, do we experience true joy.

Velma Ruch, 119-120

**PRAYER:** Homeless
Lord of us prodigal children,
how long I lived not knowing
the shelter of your love.
How bare-boned had my spirit grown
before I sat at your table
and broke bread
and drank you in.

In starless nights
as I huddled for warmth around the barrels
burning with disbelief,
quietly as a falling leaf you came:
bearing a single spark
from a different fire.

Keeper of the holy hearth,
may that spark in each of us,
kindle till it blazes white.
Warm us with your gift of fire
until love's eternal light
extinguishes the night
and we are welcomed home.

Phyllis Price, *Holy Fire*

# THE FIFTH MONDAY OF EASTER: GRACE

**The Gift:**

Amazing grace, how sweet the sound,
That saved a wretch like me!
I once was lost but now am found,
Was blind but now I see.

The Lord has promised good to me;
His word my hope secures;
He will my shield and portion be
As long as life endures.

John Newton, *Hymns of the Saints,* No. 104

**SCRIPTURE:** **2 Corinthians 6:1-2 Now Is the Acceptable Time**

*As we work together with him, we urge you also not to accept the grace of God in vain. For he says, 'At an acceptable time I have listened to you, and on a day of salvation I have helped you.' See, now is the acceptable time; see, now is the day of salvation.*

**Acts 4:33 Great Grace Was Upon Them All**

*With great power the apostles gave their testimony to the resurrection of the Lord Jesus, and great grace was upon them all.*

**2 Corinthians 13:3 A Blessing from Paul**

*The grace of the Lord Jesus Christ, the love of God, and the communion of the Holy Spirit be with all of you.*

**2 Corinthians 12:7-9. "My Grace Is Sufficient"**

*Therefore, to keep me from being too elated, a thorn was given me in the flesh, a messenger of Satan to torment me to keep me from being too elated. Three times I appealed to the Lord about this, that it would leave me, but he said to me, "My grace is sufficient for you, for power is made perfect in weakness." So I will boast all the more gladly of my weaknesses, so that the power of Christ may dwell in me.*

**MEDITATION: Spiritual Formation through Grace**

In a time when user-friendly religious communities have lost their distinct identity amid a maze of relativisms, the study of grace takes on new urgency and decisive meaning. We are the generation that has tried to massage worshiping communities into existence by using organizational finesse. We have sought to induce spirituality through strategies, to coax spiritual growth by design. Spiritual formation has been thought of like painting by numbers, as if all it takes is five fingers, twelve steps, and three colors of paint ...Grace works silently, inwardly, without publicity, like seeds underground ... Lacking grace, the task of personal growth turns into a frantic search for innovative strategies ...We have tried to

> manufacture spiritual growth while missing the very grace that would enable it. We have wanted to produce results without a readiness to receive help through the available means of grace—prayer, scripture, study, sacrament and actively serving love.
>
> --Thomas Oden, *The Transforming Power of Grace* (Nashville: Abingdon Press, 1993) 19

**The Movement of Grace in Our Lives**

The initial operation of grace in our lives has been called prevenient grace. Prevenient means "to come before." It is the first direct movement of the Divine in our lives. Prevenient grace opens us to desire. It creates a longing in us for that fuller life represented by the Spirit. Hymn No. 213 in *Hymns of the Saints* expresses this process so well:

> I sought the Lord, and afterward I knew
> He moved my soul to seek him, seeking me.
> It was not I that found, O Savior true;
> No; I was found of thee.
>
> Anonymous

The Spirit not only gives but enables us to receive the gift. It softens the "stony" of the heart as Adam said in Milton's *Paradise Lost.* He said that *after* the Fall, after he had learned a thing or two. Prevenient grace is always of such a nature that it can be negated through human will. Prevenient grace is an invitation – Christ stands at the door and knocks – but not all open the door. As Psalm 95:7 admonishes us, "*Today, if you hear his voice, do not harden your hearts*" (NIV). Even if we do harden our hearts the Spirit does not cease to summon us in an untold number of ways.

I have used the terms "grace" and "Spirit" interchangeably. It is difficult to distinguish the two though the emphasis may fall somewhat differently. Hebrews 10:29 speaks of the "Spirit of grace." Thomas C. Oden in his book, *The Transforming Power of Grace* writes,

> Grace is an overarching term for all of God's gifts to humanity, all the blessings of salvation, all events through which are manifested God's own self-giving. Grace is a Divine attribute revealing the heart of the one God, the premise of all spiritual blessing ...It is the divine disposition to work in our hearts, wills, and actions, so as actively to communicate God's self-giving love for humanity.

If we respond to the unearned gift of grace, the Spirit cooperates with us in an enabling way. It is the power that Christ promised to those who received him. While the gift is free, it calls for interactive relationship and that requires considerable effort and initiative on our parts. Beyond that, it can lead to increasing responsibility. For that reason, Scott Peck writes in *The Road Less Traveled,* many refuse the offer:

> For the call to grace is a promotion, a call to a position of higher responsibility and power. To be aware of grace, to personally experience its constant presence, to know one's nearness to God, is to know and continually experience an inner tranquility and peace that few possess.

On the other hand, this knowledge and awareness brings with it an enormous responsibility. For to experience one's closeness to God is also to experience the obligation to be God, to be the agent of his power and love. The call to grace is a call to a life of effortful caring, to a life of service and whatever sacrifice seems required. It is a call out of spiritual childhood into adulthood, a call to be a parent unto mankind (301-302).

--Velma Ruch *The Transforming Power of Prayer,* Vol. 1, 28-30

"Grace is a gift of God's own presence, and it is God's own presence that we need in us in order to keep the commandments."

Anthony Chavala Smith

**Grace in Communal Conflict**

The movements of God's grace in the midst of communal conflict are often subtle. They generate no headlines. In our division-obsessed age, they rarely even give rise to rumors that something hopeful is happening. Nevertheless, when a clear definition of issues starts to replace confusion, that is a movement of grace. When one side begins to understand the genuine fears, desires, and gifts of the other, God's healing grace is active. This is so even if the two sides remain far apart in their views.

I am convinced that wherever we live with division in our communities of faith, we need to pray for sensitivity to the movements of God's grace among us. And whenever we see such movements, we need to name them and give thanks. We need to do this not to engage in some simplistic act of looking on the bright side. We need to do it in faithfulness to the One who has said, "*I am about to do a new thing: now it springs forth, do you not perceive it?*" (Isaiah 43:19) and again has said, "*See, I am making all things new*" (Revelation 21:5). To pray that we be sensitive to the movement of God's grace is to look squarely into the pain of our own divisions. It is to ask that precisely in this pain we may discover how the Loving One is forming us anew.

--Stephen V. Doughty, "How Do We Pray When We Are Divided?" *Weavings* (July/August 2003): 44-45.

**PRAYER:** I am trusting thee, Lord, Jesus; At they feet I bow.
For thy grace and tender mercy, Lord, we trust thee now.

I am trusting thee to guide me; Thou alone shalt lead,
Every day and hour supplying All that I may need.

I am trusting thee, Lord Jesus; Never let me fall;
I am trusting thee forever, Thrusting thee for all. Amen.

Frances Ridley Havergal, *Hymns of the Saints,* No. 127

# THE FIFTH TUESDAY OF EASTER: PRAYER

**The Discipline of Prayer:**

Meditation introduces us to the inner life, fasting is an accompanying means, but it is the discipline of prayer itself that brings us into the deepest and highest work of the human spirit. Real prayer is life creating and life changing

Richard Foster, *Celebration of Discipline.*

**SCRIPTURE:** **Matthew 7:7-8 Ask, Search, and Knock**

*"Ask, and it will be given you; search, and you will find; knock, and the door will be opened for you. For everyone who asks receives, and everyone who searches finds, and for everyone who knocks, the door will be opened."*

**Romans 8:26-27 The Spirit Intercedes**

*Likewise the Spirit helps us in our weakness; for we do not know how to pray as we ought, but that very Spirit intercedes with sighs too deep for words. And God, who searches the heart, knows what is the mind of the Spirit, because the Spirit intercedes for the saints according to the will of God.*

**MEDITATION: Stages in the Life of Prayer**

Consider Christ's three promises of prayer: "Ask, and it shall be given you; seek, and you will find; knock, and the door will be opened for you. For everone who asks receives, and everyone who searches finds, and for everyone the door will be opened." Note how all of them are attached to something done by us. The question of whether we will commune with God is left to us, to the freedom of our wills. God gives out of his treasury what we really ask, seek, and long for. His supply is infinite; it is our demands which are shallow, mistrustful, and vague. The saints were so sure about the extent in which human life is a spiritual thing and Spirit-fed that they asked and received much.

*"Ask," "seek," and "knock;"* there is something very definite about that. Those words represent three very real stages in the life of prayer corresponding to a steady growth and enrichment of the soul's encounter with God. When we begin in prayer, all of us feel very helpless. We are filled with craving and longing. We are asking for God. We want assurance, light, spiritual food, strength to carry on and deal with our difficulties and sins ...Opening our souls to the spiritual world in prayer, *asking, we do receive* –although, perhaps not instantly or sensationally. Perhaps the answer is not exactly what we expect. Still a gift is made, and prayer in the spiritual life becomes possible to us.

The second promise is that if we will seek, we will find. That meditation which is a deep brooding exploration and thinking in God's presence is a way to the real discoveries of the spiritual life. ...Yielding ourselves to God in prayer, gradually discovering bit by bit, often not in big disclosures, is his call to our souls ...The Church is not a society of specialists, but of living, loving, ever-growing souls which must stretch up to God in adoration and out to one's companions in active love...One of the great functions of prayer is to train us to this attitude of soul Seeking his will requires courage, patience, and trust. The deep things of prayer are first given in response to these ...Seeking God in prayer means we have realized that we want Him more than any of His gifts.

For the third promise we are asked to knock. Now comes the time in our prayer when we seem brought up short by a closed door. Generally, we experience the other side of that door, the riches of the house of God. But this is the real life at which all our education in prayer has been gently aiming, life lived in the atmosphere of God beyond entreaty and search. We leave those off when we are at home.

> *Knock.* Nothing is said about what happens when the door opens. Christ's silence is more eloquent than speech. We needn't suppose that other sorts of prayer are then shut to us. Saint John said that the sheep come in and out of the door and find pasture. Adoration brings us to a door, but it is life in the world beyond the door that then overrules all ...Thus we learn to weave together this world and the Eternal World, and we fill all we do with gentle loveliness which is of God.
>
> Evelyn Underhill, "Breathing the Air of Eternity," *Weavings* (May/June 2002*)*: -11; used with permission

**The Gift of Prayer**

Prayer is perhaps the deepest impulse of the human soul and our fundamental spiritual activity. We have heard many times, "There are no atheists in foxholes." In times of crisis even the so-called non-religious almost instinctively turn to prayer. Beyond that, prayer is an expression of the hunger of the human soul for home, for something stable amidst the fluctuation of human life. The prayer for which we seek, however, is not just the instinctive reaction in time of danger or confusion, but rather prayer as true communion with the Divine. What is at stake is immediate spiritual fellowship with the Divine. It is, as Harry Emerson Fosdick once wrote, "the loftiest experience within the reach of any soul."

The reality and power of prayer can only be verified by praying. A recognition of that reality emerges out of experience. All the arguments in the world will not convince any one of that reality if the person has not himself or herself discovered what communion with God really means. Those who have can never be shaken by arguments purporting the unreality of that presence. They know beyond doubt of its presence but their affirmations are marked by deep humility because they recognize that what has been experienced is only the smallest glimpses of what can be. What happens in prayer is finally lost in mystery.

The healthiness and growth in our prayer journey depends to a great extent on the suppleness and variety we are able to bring to it – sometimes speaking, public or private, sometimes listening, sometimes thinking, sometimes resting in the communion which is beyond thought or speech but always ready for the surprise that can come when we are touched even with the lightness of a butterfly wing. It is important for us, as Evelyn Underhill has written, to "find out the kind of practice that suits our souls; -- yours, not someone else's and now at this stage of its growth. You have to find and develop the prayer that fully employs you and yet does not overstrain you; the prayer in which you are quite supple before God; the prayer that refreshes, braces and expands you, and is best able to carry you over the inevitable fluctuations of spiritual level and mood."

What prayer requires is a daily, hourly state of attention, a being alert and aware, a predisposition to be aware of God in all things. How we express that awareness varies greatly. Richard Foster in his book *Prayer* explores that infinite variety. Prayer comes to us in varying degrees of intensity. In our moments of subtlest awareness we may sense God as so pervasive that all specific content disappears. This is sometimes referred to as contemplative prayer and is a gift, as all true prayer is. Though our personal preparation and readiness are involved the wordless communion that develops can only be given us by the Holy Spirit.

One such experience came to me one Sunday morning as I was driving back on icy roads from our little country church at Andover. Lamoni Stake was in the midst of a preaching series by Brother J. C. Stuart on the theme "The Bush Still Burns." On Friday night when the series began we were hit with a terrible ice storm. On Sunday morning I was scheduled to give the communion talk at Andover. The roads were still a glare of ice and getting to Andover was risky indeed. I did make it as did a few others and we had a good service. But it was after the service, as I was driving back that the miracle happened. Still in the mood of the service and still on icy roads, I found myself enveloped in peace and deep joy. I recognized that presence though it was unaccompanied by any words from me or from the Divine. There was no need for words. It was the experience of oneness that lifts us beyond the realm of the mundane into a whole new atmosphere of being. The experience in its intensity lasted for perhaps half an hour, even while I was eating alone in the restaurant with a hubbub of voices around me. I was not unaware of those others. I looked at them with eyes of wonder and love. The experience faded, though it was accompanied by the afterglow of assurance of the love that is at the center of our universe. One such experience is enough to convince us of the knowledge that is beyond knowledge.

The wonder in prayer, though a gift of the Spirit, needs to be prepared for. It is to help us in that preparation that intentional spiritual formation is of such value in our lives and why these scriptures and meditations are shared with you. May they indeed lift you into the presence of the Divine.

Velma Ruch

**PRAYER:** Loving God, our comfort and guide, without you we would be very much alone as we meet the challenges of life. With you, we can be whole and strong even in the most difficult of circumstances. But the greatest gift you have given us is the possibility of having heart to heart communion with you. With that gift we can never despair or feel bereft of companionship. We do not belittle the meaningful relationship we have with our brothers and sisters as we journey together, but it is the love you have planted in our hearts that is the bond that ties us all together. With joy we offer to you our gratitude and praise and pray that your Spirit in us may reach out in blessing to others. Amen.

# THE FIFTH WEDNESDAY OF EASTER: PRACTICING THE PRESENCE

**Invocation:**

May thy presence be ours in full measure.
Let thy spirit abide without end.
With thy love as our hearts' greatest treasure,
We will praise thee our Lord and our friend.

Adapted from the Russian, *Hymns of the Saints,* No. 102

**SCRIPTURE:** **Psalm 46:10 Be Still and Know**

*"Be still and know that I am God."*

**Book of Mormon, Alma 17:69-70 Learn Wisdom in Youth**

*O remember, my son and learn wisdom in your youth; learn in your youth to keep the commandments of God and cry to God for all your support Let all your doings be unto the Lord, and wherever you go, let it be in the Lord; let the affections of your heart be placed upon the Lord forever; counsel with the Lord in all your doings, and he will direct you for good. When you lie down at night, lie down unto the Lord, that he may watch over you in your sleep; and when you rise in the morning, let your heart be full of thanks to God; and if you do these things, you shall be lifted up in the last day.*

**MEDITATION: Practicing the Presence**

What we are aiming for in the spiritual discipline most closely related to the incarnational life is what Brother Lawrence in the seventeenth century called "practicing the presence" and what Paul meant when he wrote "*Pray without ceasing*" (1 Thessalonians. 5:17) It is to recognize every experience as a transparency of God. It is a sharing in the life of the vine. The person that does not so share is like a branch that is broken and withers away. The one who does is living the incarnational life.

We learn much by studying Brother Lawrence's experiences as told in his own words (see *Practicing the Presence,* ed. Gene Edwards [Auburn, Maine: Christian Books, 1976]). Brother Lawrence was a humble man. He was originally a footman but as he himself wrote, he was awkward and tended to break everything. In what seemed failure he decided to join a monastery where he thought God might punish him for his failures and help him become a better man. He was assigned to work in the kitchen, something he originally disliked but which became a means of his making the love of God his All. He practiced many spiritual disciplines but none of them seemed to do for him what was needed. Finally, he decided that the shortest way to God is "to go straight to him by a continual exercise of love and doing all things for his sake." Doing this did not happen automatically and there were times of deep despair. But at those times he prayed God for forgiveness and tried again. Finally he discovered that the set times of prayer prescribed by the monastery were no different from any other part of his day. He became aware of the presence of the Divine in himself, in all things he did, and in his relationship to others. All of his life and action emerged from a love of God and resulted in a joy that no hardship or suffering could alter.

**A Divine Center**

Life is meant to be lived from a Center, a divine Center. Each one of us can live such a life of amazing power and peace and serenity, of integration and confidence and simplified multiplicity, on one condition – that is, *if we really want to.* There is a divine abyss within us all, a holy Infinite Center, a Heart, a Life who speaks in us and through us to the world. We have all heard this holy Whisper at times. At times we have followed the Whisper, and amazing equilibrium of life, amazing effectiveness of living set in. But too many of us have heeded the Voice only at times. Only at times have we submitted to His holy guidance. We have not counted this Holy Thing within us to be the most precious thing in the world. We have not surrendered *all else,* to attend to it alone …

Many of the things we are doing seem so important to us. We haven't been able to say No to them, because they seemed so important. But if we *center down,* as the old phrase goes, and live in that holy Silence which is dearer than life, and take our life program into the silent places of the heart, with complete openness, ready to do, ready to renounce according to His leading, then many of the things we are doing lose their vitality for us. I should like to testify to this, as a personal experience, graciously given. There is a reevaluation of much that we do or try to do, which is *done for us,* and we know what to do and what to let alone.

Do you want to live in such an amazing divine Presence that life is transformed and transfigured and transmuted into peace and power and glory and miracle? If you do, then you can …With delight I read Brother Lawrence, in his *Practice of the Presence of God.* At the close of the Fourth Conversation it is reported of him, "He was never hasty nor loitering, but did each thing in its season, with an even uninterrupted composure and tranquility of spirit. "The time of business,' he said, 'does not with me differ from the time of prayer, and in the noise and clatter of my kitchen, while several persons are at the same time calling for different things, I possess God in as great tranquility as if I were upon my knees at the blessed sacrament.'" Our real problem, in failing to center down, is not a lack of time; it is, I fear, in too many of us, lack of joyful, enthusiastic delight in Him, lack of deep, deep-drawing love directed toward Him at every hour of the day and night.

I think it is clear that I am talking about a revolutionary way of living. Religion isn't something to be added to our other duties, and thus make our lives yet more complex. The life with God is the center of life, and all else is remodeled and integrated by it. It gives the singleness of eye. The most important thing is not to be perpetually passing out cups of cold water to a thirsty world. We can get so fearfully busy trying to carry out the second great commandment "*Thou shalt love thy neighbor as thyself,*" that we are under-developed in our devoted love to God …The deepest need of men is not food and clothing and shelter, important as they are. It is God. We have mistaken the nature of poverty and thought it was economic poverty. No, it is poverty of soul, deprivation of God's recreating, loving peace …

> Life from the Center is a life of unhurried peace and power. It is simple. It is serene. It is amazing. It is triumphant. It is radiant. It takes no time, but it occupies all our time. And it makes our life programs new and overcoming. We need not get frantic. He is at the helm. And when our little day is done we lie down quietly in peace, for all is well.

Excerpts from Thomas R. Kelly, *A Testament of Devotion,* 116-124; used with permission

PRAYER:

Draw thou my soul, O Christ, Closer to thine;
Breathe into every wish Thy will divine.
Raised my low self above, Won by thy deathless love,
Ever, O Christ, through mine, Let thy life shine.

Lead forth my soul, O Christ, One with thine own;
Joyful to follow thee Through paths unknown.
In thee my strength renew; Give me thy work to do,
Through me thy truth be shown, Thy love made known.

Not for myself alone May my prayer be;
Lift thou thy world, O Christ, Closer to thee;
Cleanse it of guilt and wrong; Teach it salvation's song,
Till earth, as heaven, fulfills God's holy will. Amen.

Lucy Larcom, *Hymns of the Saints*, No. 168

# THE FIFTH THURSDAY OF EASTER: FRUITS OF THE SPIRIT

**Admonition:**

**Sanctify yourselves that your minds become single to God, and the days will come that you shall see him; for he will unveil his face unto you, and it shall be in his own time, and in his own way, and according to his own will**

*(D. and C. 85:18b).*

**SCRIPTURE:** **Galatians 5:22-23 The Fruit of the Spirit**

*The fruit of the Spirit is love, joy, peace, patience, kindness, goodness, faithfulness, gentleness and self-control.*

**John 15:16 Chosen to Bear Fruit**

*You have not chosen me, but I have chosen you, and ordained you that you should go and bring forth fruit, and that your fruit should remain.*

**MEDITATION: Love, Joy, Peace**

Just as it is natural for a tree to bear fruit, it is natural in response to faith that the fruits of the Spirit will develop. Evelyn Underhill both in her books and retreat presentations, emphasized the first three fruits of the Spirit mentioned in Galatians: *love, joy, and peace:*

> They are the signature of the Spirit of Christ in the soul and the originating cause of all other spiritual fruits: longsuffering, gentleness, goodness, faith, meekness, and temperance. No really good life of any kind is ever really done unless it is done in love, joy, and peace.
>
> *The Ways of the Spirit*, 59-60

Being rooted and grounded in love is the first requisite, and out of it grow joy and peace.

Through the writings of Paul we learn that perfect consecration brings joy. This is particularly manifest in his letter to the Philippians. Ron James titled his commentary on Philippians *A Joy Wider Than the World* and writes,

> What is indispensable to the experience of joy is to be "taken out of the self"; to allow one's own center to be apprehended by that which is beyond it, addresses it, appeals to it, and by its touch leaves a pang of inconsolable longing. The task then, in the words of Robert Louis Stevenson, is "to find out where joy resides, and give it a voice far beyond singing. For to miss the joy is to miss all (127).

That union with God that satisfies our deepest yearning begins in love, leads to joy, and gives us peace. Peace, serenity at the very base of being, is one of the surest indications of life lived in Christ. "That deep tranquility which we mean by peace of soul," Evelyn Underhill wrote,

> is the surest of all signs of spiritual health. Its calm atmosphere must enwrap our love and our joy if that love and joy are to…work God's will. A peacefulness which persists through success and through suffering alike is the real mark of the Christian soul (71).
>
> We have often enough seen those spiritual giants among us who can become the instruments of God in changing the environment of which they are a part and inaugurating a whole new line of march. So it was with the apostles at Pentecost and after. In the fifty days between the Resurrection and Pentecost they were changed from somewhat frail and inconstant individuals to apostolic witnesses. What had happened was that the love they had received from Christ and the peace he had promised were infused with Power. Christ had told them it would be so. The first few chapters of Acts are among the most inspiring in the New Testament. They give us hope that the power once given will be with us forever and will grow in us as we are responsive to the Spirit that works within.
>
> --Velma Ruch, *The Transforming Power of Prayer*, Vol. 1, 178-182

The theme of transformation has been running through most of these meditations. Transformation is not possible unless we daily live in such a way that the fruits of the Spirit can be manifest in us. Deborah Smith Douglas has written,

> We all long to be changed. Ancient traditions are brimful of songs and stories of metamorphosis, of transformation. We seem to be born with what the poet Emily Dickinson called "a dim capacity for wings." Our culture notoriously capitalizes on that longing, pandering to our basic insecurities and insisting that we can be different (richer, smarter, healthier, more popular, stronger, more successful) if we only spend more money on self-improvement products and schemes. But far beneath that noisy, crowded, superficial level of our lives – the level accessible to Hollywood and Madison Avenue – our desire for transformation runs deep and strong as an underground river.
>
> That desire is at the heart of our faith. It is the fundamental assumption of our sacramental theology: Baptism and Eucharist both speak of our yearning to be born again, to be re-made, to become living members of the Body of Christ, to be part of the new creation. Our desire for God – and God's desire for us – is basic to our human nature, and to our spiritual lives, and is inextricably bound up with a desire to be changed.
>
> Nevertheless, almost as deep in us as our yearning to be changed, to be delivered from "this body of death," is our resistance to our own transformation Over and over again, we lock God out. We cover our ears. We blind ourselves to the divine transformational opportunities that stand before us … The story of the healing pool of Bethzatha in the gospel of John is a story of that kind of complicated longing, a yearning for wholeness that nonetheless almost doesn't see what has been offered, doesn't understand what has been given (see John 5:1-18) …

Attachment to our own grievances and expectations ("I never get to be first;there is no one to help me") can act as a powerful barrier to the abundant life God longs to give us. Even more perilously, we can become so attached to our own need to be right, and to be in control that we place ourselves outside the longing for change that might open us to God.

By grace, God's longing for our wholeness is more powerful than our expectations or our need for control. By grace, God does not wait until we know the depth or our need or awaken to the strength of our need to be right. By grace, God comes to us in the high tide of our grievances, in the full flowering of our certainties, and asks in ways most suited to our condition, "Do you want to be healed?"

Deborah Smith Douglas, "Do You Want to Be Healed," *Weavings* (September/October 1995): 19-24; used with permission

The question, "Do you want to be healed? haunts us all. We think we really do, but healing means change and we are not always willing to pay the price for that healing. One way to begin is to practice personal disciplines. We are all in the process of becoming. The question we must continually ask ourselves is, "Is my life on the right track?" In the presence of the Master we are completely transparent. We become aware of how far we are from being what we were created to be. Something deep in us really wants to change. The personal disciplines can help us in growing into a life of holiness, of developing the fruits of the Spirit. The process involves first the seeing, then the willing and finally submission to a power greater than our own. We are working to remove the layers that bind us so we can arise in newness of life. The process is multifaceted. It may involve fasting, controlling our thinking, watching our speaking, confessing, being willing to change, cultivating integrity in all we do, practicing "Holy Leisure," taking time for rest and release of stress, giving and receiving forgiveness, and on and on. The process is not easy and we have to proceed prayerfully. In the Spirit-inhabited deeps that develop the fruits of the Spirit grow. Just as it is natural for a tree to bear fruit, it is natural in response to faith that the fruits of the Spirit will develop. Are you willing to commit yourself to such discipline? Do you *want* to be healed?

**PRAYER:** Yes, God, we really do want to be healed but there are so many barriers, both self-imposed and imposed upon us by others, that we often falter and give up. We know without you and your constant grace in our lives we will allow opportunities for change to pass us by. In this hour of contrition we ask your forgiveness and once again open our hearts and minds to give you room to dwell in us. Give us grace to follow, we pray. Amen.

# THE FIFTH FRIDAY OF EASTER: GIFTS OF THE SPIRIT

It is important for us to recognize the difference between fruits of the Spirit and gifts of the Spirit. Spiritual fruit has to do with our relationships and the spiritual quality of our lives. Spiritual gifts, on the other hand, have to do with our calling and our function in ministry. Spiritual fruits relate to what we are; spiritual gifts to what we do. In a very important way fruits of the Spirit become the soil out of which the gifts can emerge. That was essentially what Paul was saying in that great 13th chapter of Corinthians. Whatever gifts we have tend to become limited to in scope if we do not have love and added to love, faith and hope.

**SCRIPTURE:** **1 Peter 4:10 Each Has A Gift**

*As each has received a gift, even so minister to one another, as good stewards of the manifold grace of God.*

**1 Corinthians 12:1-11 Gifts for the Common Good**

*Now concerning spiritual gifts, brothers and sisters, I do not want you to be uninformed ... Now there are varieties of gifts, but the same Spirit, and there are varieties of services, but the same Lord;... To each is given the manifestation of the Spirit for the common good.*

**1 Corinthians 13 The Greatest of These Is Love**

*If I speak in the tongues of mortals and of angels, but do not have love, I am a noisy gong or a clanging cymbal. And if I have prophetic powers and understand all mysteries and all knowledge, and if I have all faith, so as to remove mountains, but do not have love, I am nothing.*

**Romans 12:6-7 Gifts that Differ**

*We have gifts that differ according to the grace given to us: prophecy in proportion to faith; ministry in ministering; the teacher in teaching; the exhorter in exhortation; the giver, in generosity; the leader in diligence; the compassionate in cheerfulness.*

**Book of Mormon, Moroni 10:8-14. The Gifts Are Many**

*And again I exhort you...that ye deny not the gifts of God, for they are many, and they come from the same God. And there are different ways that these gifts are administered; but it is the same God who worketh all in all; and they are given by the manifestations of the Spirit of God unto men, to profit them.*

**Doctrine and Covenants 46:4-7 Selective Gifts**

*And again, verily I say unto you, I would that ye should always remember, and always retain in your minds what those gifts are that are given unto the church, for all have not every gift given unto them.*

**MEDITATION: All Are Called**

All are called according to the gifts of God unto them. That is a basic belief of the church. It is saying that we all share responsibility for carrying on the work of the church. God intends that the ministry of the church be accomplished through spiritual gifts. Human talents in and of themselves are not adequate for spiritual ministry. Paul declared: *"Weak men we may be, but it is not as such we fight our battles. The weapons we wield are not merely human, but divinely potent to demolish strongholds"* (2 Cor. 10:3-4 New English Bible). Nothing less than the blessings and resources of the Divine will equip the church to meet the opportunities of this generation.

Discovering our call is a life-time process. We may know fairly early in our lives the general direction of the call, but we change, circumstances change and we may find that we are called to serve in different ways. Still there is likely to be a growing conviction of a central call.

A gift is a gift is a gift but is subject to discipline. We do not decide what gifts will be ours. It is a gift of the Spirit and subject to the Spirit's will. The discovery of our spiritual gifts is important because that leads us into the necessary discipline to enhance the gifts. One way to prepare and go about discovering is asking each day, "What does God want of me this day?" It helps us set priorities. A help in answering this question is asking another, "Where is my deepest joy? In what activity do I find fulfillment? What are the special moments in my life?" That which brings us joy is an avenue to fulfillment that needs to be cultivated. One writer attempted to answer the question for all of us by saying, "My deepest joy comes in using the gifts God has given me to do the divine work in the world. It is doing something well and feeling fulfilled in doing it." A number of psychologists are coming to a similar conclusion. One started by trying to discover why it was that so many people lived miserable lives. That led him to look at the question from another point of view. "What is it that distinguishes people that live fulfilled lives?" He came to the conclusion that it involved satisfying work. It is a sense that we have a purpose for our existence and we and we are alert to those occasions where we can give it our best expression.

Can you identify your own source of joy? In all of the activities in which you engage where do you find the greatest satisfaction? Is there in your own mind a relationship between that satisfaction and your spiritual giftedness?

Ponder the scriptures on the gifts. What have you learned from them that could apply to your own life or your congregation?

**PRAYER:** Help us express your love, O Lord,
Committed to one world in thee!
Abundant gifts enhance our lives;
Oh, free them for humanity.

There is no season when we dare
Withhold our love from humankind.
Embracing earth's supporting strength,
We match whatever needs we find.

The grace of God can flood the heart,
Give love its fullness and its glow;
Our unconfined and free delight
Springs forth impelled by nature's flow. Amen.

Cleo Hanthorne Moon, *Hymns of the Saints,* No. 415

# THE FIFTH SATURDAY OF EASTER: WITNESSING: I HAVE CHOSEN YOU

**Take Time To Be Holy:**

**Begin! Fix some part of every day for private exercise ...Whether you like it or no, read and pray daily. It is for your life; there is no other way; else you will be a trifler all your days...Do justice to your own soul; give it time and means to grow. Do not starve yourself any longer**

(John Wesley).

**SCRIPTURE:** **John 15:16-17 I Chose You!**

*"You did not choose me but I chose you. And I anointed you to go and bear fruit, fruit that will last, so that the Father will give you whatever you ask him in my name. I am giving you these commands so that you may love one another.*

**Matthew 27:19-20 Make Disciples of All Nations**

*"Go therefore and make disciples of all nations, baptizing them in the name of the Father and of the Son and of the Holy Spirit, and teaching them to obey everything that I have commanded you. And remember, I am with you always, to the end of the age.*

**MEDITATION: Oil for Our Lamps**

Recently as I was reading through the Gospel of Luke I was struck by the statement in the twelfth chapter: "*Be dressed for action and have your lamps lit.*" The passage in Luke goes on, "*Be like those who are waiting for their master to return from the wedding banquet, so that they may open the door for him as soon as he comes and knocks.*" We can read this passage as a reference to the Second Coming, but more important for us this day is to hear it as God's summons to each of us. We have all known those moments when eternity invades time and calls us to respond. There is work to be done.

It is both an intimidating and exalting moment when we answer the knock at the door of our spirit and hear the words, "*I have chosen you. Go and bear fruit.*" Are we ready for such a call? Are we dressed for action with our lamps lit or are we more like the five virgins who had forgotten to replenish the oil in their lamps and so did not have the spiritual reserves to allow them to respond. Have you been there? Or had your light already begun to flicker in preparation for dying out altogether? Were you perhaps so unprepared that you were oblivious to the fact that anything out of the ordinary had happened? Were you, and that includes us all, so cynical and uncomprehending that you resisted this call to rise above yourself? Had you, perhaps taken so few steps on the pilgrim journey that you responded simplistically or with misunderstanding? On the other hand, had you grown to the point that you were aware of the mystery of God's call and could glimpse what was possible for you even if you were not there yet? Did you at any time have the courage to say yes to the call that demands the ultimate sacrifice, the transformation of self?

These invasions of the eternal into our lives come many times and at different points in our development. From the time we are born there is a persistent calling and we respond or we do not according to our willingness to listen. God is in the business of calling us from the earliest years. As we grow beyond childhood fancies and dreams, come experiences of greater magnitude when we keenly feel within ourselves what we must be and do. These are experiences of unreleased power waiting for their moment of understanding and fulfillment. Then as we continue to respond, attempting to be dressed for action with our lamps lit, we go beyond our point of apprenticeship into a time of vocational readiness. We are eager to come forth and yield ourselves fully to that to which we are called. We experience the joy of being chosen and of offering our gifts to the One who has called.

> You came down from your throne and stood at my cottage door.
> I was singing all alone in a corner, and the melody caught your ear.
> You came down and stood at my cottage door.
> Masters are many in your hall, and songs are sung there at all hours.
> But the simple carol of this novice struck at your love. One plaintive
> little strain mingled with the great music of the world, and with a flower
> for a prize you came down and stopped at my cottage door.
>
> Rabindranath Tagore, *Gitanjali, Poem 49*

An experience such as Tagore writes about is indeed humbling. It is difficult to imagine that the God of all the universe finds delight in our singing, in what we have to give. But God from our earliest days has come to us calling us into a future that only experience can verify. I had such an experience in a Christmas service in the Chariton, Iowa congregation. I was the evangelist assigned to that congregation and I went that day not to preach but just to be with the people. At the end of the service presented by the youth of the congregation they came to each of us and presented a Christmas greeting and a flower. I was sitting there smiling, enjoying the scene, when a young girl handed me a simple, artificial flower. At that moment I was taken by surprise by an overwhelming sense of God's presence and tears began to stream down my face. I tried to control my emotion because I thought the people would not know why I was crying. But as that flower was handed to me it was more than just a small, red flower. It was the presence of Christ. I felt like Tagore "And with a flower for a prize, he came down and stood at my cottage door." More than that, as the love of the Divine touched me, my heart was filled with love for the young girl who handed it to me. She was a messenger of the Lord, also touched by his love, and it was to her and to others like her I was called to minister.

When we respond to the call of God, however it comes, it is like a command performance, an opportunity to give of our best to the Lord of the Universe. When we do, what happens next is amazing. We ourselves are purified in the process and experience the joy for which we were created. It is of that joy that Tagore also wrote:

When thou commandest me to sing it seems that my heart would
break with pride; and I look to thy face, and tears come to my eyes.
All that is harsh and dissonant in my life melts into one sweet harmony –
And my adoration spreads wings like a glad bird on its flight across the sea.
I know thou taketh pleasure in my singing. I know that only as a singer
I come before thy presence.
I touch the edge of the far spreading wing of my song thy feet which I
never could aspire to reach.
Drunk with the joy of singing I forget myself and call thee friend who
art my Lord.

Gitanjali, Poem 2

**PRAYER:** O Thou, Who art the God no less of those who know thee not as of those who love thee well, be present with us at the times of choosing when time stands still and all that lies behind and all that lies ahead are caught up in the mystery of a moment. Be present especially with the young who must choose between many voices. Help them to know that there are words of truth and healing that will never be spoken unless they speak them, and deeds of compassion and courage that will never be done unless they do them. Help them never to take success for victory or failure for defeat. Grant that they may never be entirely content with whatever bounty the world may bestow upon them, but that they may know at last that they were created not for happiness but for joy, and that joy is to those alone who, sometimes with tears in their eyes, commit themselves in love to thee and to their brothers and sisters. Lead them and all thy world ever deeper into the knowledge that finally all persons are one and that there can never really be joy for any until there is joy for all. In Christ's name we ask it and for his sake. Amen.

Frederick Buechner, *The Hungering Dark*
(HarperSanFrancisco, 1969), 32-33

# THE SIXTH WEEK OF EASTER THEME: THE SPIRIT'S TRANSFORMING TOUCH

## THE SIXTH SUNDAY OF EASTER: MARY, THE MOTHER OF JESUS

**God's Instrument:**

O Lord, open my eyes that I may see the need of others, open my ears that I may hear their cries, open my heart so that they need not be without succour, let me be not afraid to defend the weak because of the anger of the strong, nor afraid to defend the poor because of the anger of the rich. Show me where love and hope and faith are needed, and use me to bring them to those places. And so open my eyes and my ears that I may this coming day be able to do some work of peace for thee

(Selection from Alan Paton).

**SCRIPTURE:** **Luke 1:46-56 The Magnificat**

And Mary said, "My soul magnifies the Lord, and my spirit rejoices in God my Savior, for he has looked with favor on the lowliness of his servant. Surely from now on all generations will call me blessed; for the Mighty One has done great things for me, and holy is his name. His mercy is for those who fear him from generation to generation.

**MEDITATION: Mary, A Woman for Our Time**

Some years ago one of the pillars of Marian piety was a book titled *A Woman Wrapped in Silence.* In that book Mary came across as remote and ethereal, unreal, and unreachable. She swept on and off its pages in gossamer and shawl. She was docile and bowed and passive. Strong in suffering, yes, but not like women who had to bend their wits to live, bear, and survive. Not like women who gave their entire lives for the salvation of others.

Mary was portrayed simply as a pawn in the will of God. But a "pawn in the will of God" is a contradiction in terms. There simply cannot be a "pawn in the will of God." The will of God is something that must be chosen and that costs. The will of God is not a trick played on the unsuspecting. The will of God is always an offer of co-creation. Mary was asked, and Mary said yes.

It wasn't that Mary was "a woman wrapped in silence." It was simply that her actions spoke more loudly than any number of words could ever do.

We, all of us, women and men, need to understand those actions now. The fact is that Mary is not simply "Mary, the mother of God." No, on the contrary, the mother of God is the image of women everywhere. The mother of God is Mary, independent woman; Mary, the unmarried mother; Mary, the homeless woman; Mary the political refugee. Mary, the Third World woman; Mary, the mother of the condemned; Mary the widow who outlives her child; Mary, the woman of our time who shares in the divine plan of salvation; Mary, the bearer of Christ.

Mary could withstand and confront every standard of her synagogue and of her society and take the poverty, the oppression, and the pain that resulted, because the will of God meant more to her than the laws of any system. That's the kind of woman God chose to do God's work. That's the kind of woman the church raises up for women to be. That's the woman who made the Magnificat the national anthem of women everywhere.

Indeed God was with her. And because of Mary, God is also with us. How can we possibly do less.

Joan Chittister, "Yesterday's Dangerous Vision," *Sojourners* (July 1987): 21; reprinted with permission from *Sojourners* magazine, www.sojo.net

**Are You Willing?**

When I was pursuing my doctor's degree at the University of Wisconsin, I was studying very hard in preparation for twenty hours of written exams over American and English literature. I was very tired and one night I found myself in a state of rebellion, wondering why I was putting myself through all of this. In the midst of my inner grumbling and desire to give it all up, a voice broke through my inner consciousness saying, "You are a partner in my work yet to come. What you are doing is important. Are you willing?" My heart did indeed burn as I was confronted with a question that demanded response. Without hesitation I found myself answering in the words of Mary, "*Behold the handmaid of the Lord. Be it unto me according to your will.*" Though the experience gave me peace, clarity, and direction, the thought that in that moment I was having a one on One conversation with the living God and in the process making not only a promise but a vow to the ruler of the universe goes beyond reason. But as Pascal once so eloquently expressed it, "The heart has its reasons which reason does not know." (*Pensees)* I have not forgotten and have in my small way tried to be true to my promise

PRAYER: I would be true, for there are those who trust me;
I would be pure, for there are those who care;
I would be strong for there is much to suffer;
I would be brave, for there is much to dare;

I would be friend of all, the foe, the friendless;
I would be giving, and forget the gift;
I would be humble, for I know my weakness;
I would look up and laugh and love and lift.

I would be prayerful through each busy moment;
I would be constantly in touch with God;
I would be tuned to hear his slightest whisper;
I would have faith to keep the path Christ trod.

Howard Arnold Walter, *Hymns of the Saints,* No. 404

# THE SIXTH MONDAY OF EASTER: MARY AND MARTHA

**Invocation:**

Eternal Parent, help me see
The life-proclaiming dignity,
The giftedness, the Spirit flame
In all Your children, in Your name. Amen.

Evelyn Maples, *Hymns of the Saints,* No. 432.

**SCRIPTURE:** **Luke 10:38-42 Choosing the Better Part**

*Now as they went on their way, he entered a certain village, where a woman named Martha welcomed him into her home. She had a sister named Mary, who sat at the Lord's feet and listened to what he was saying. But Martha was distracted by her many tasks; so she came to him and asked, "Lord, do you not care that my sister has left me to do all the work by myself? Tell her then to help me." But the Lord answered her, "Martha, Martha, you are worried and distracted by many things; there is need of only one thing. Mary has chosen the better part, which will not be taken away from her."*

**John 11:17-27 "You Are the Messiah, the Son of God"**

*When Jesus arrived, he found that Lazarus had already been in the tomb four days. Now Bethany was near Jerusalem, some two miles away and many of the Jews had come to Martha and Mary to console them about their brother. When Martha heard that Jesus was coming, she went and met him, while Mary stayed at home. Martha said to Jesus, "Lord, if you had been here, my brother would not have died. But even now I know that God will give you whatever you ask of him." Jesus said to her, "Your brother will rise again." Martha said to him, "I know that he will rise again in the resurrection on the last day." Jesus said to her, "I am the resurrection and the life. Those who believe in me, even though they die they will live, and everyone who lives and believes in me will never die. Do you believe this?" "Yes, Lord, I believe that you are the Messiah, the Son of God, the one coming into the world."*

**MEDITATION: Different But Equally Worthy**

Jesus was remarkable in how he appreciated and supported different temperaments and talents. The difference between Mary and Martha provide an excellent illustration of this, In her book, *The Women Around Jesus,* Elizabeth Moltman-Wendel reminds us of two stories about these sisters as recorded in Luke and John. The account we know best is the one related by Luke (10:38-42). In it Mary was sitting at the feet of Jesus, and Martha –upset over all the work she had to do—complained that Mary was not helping her. Jesus said, *"Martha, Martha, you are troubled about many things. But one thing is needful and Mary has chosen that good part which shall not be taken away from her."* As the result of this story, taken alone, we have thought of Mary as the contemplative, spiritual type and of Martha in the lesser role of the active, practical type.

The story which John chooses to tell, however, throws a different light on these two sisters (John 11). In his account Martha plays the principal role. Jesus had heard of Lazarus's illness but did not arrive to Bethany until after his friend had died. When Martha heard he was coming, she rushed out to meet him, but "Mary sat still in the house." Martha complained a little. "*Lord, if you had been here my brother would not have died.,"* but she also had faith that Christ could do something even then. He said to her, "*I am the resurrection and the life; he that believes in me, though he were dead, yet shall he live...Do you believe this?*" She responded, "*Yes, Lord, I believe that you are the Christ, the son of the living God, which shall come into the world.*" By saying this, she made a confession of the divinity of Christ very much like the one made by Peter. "*Thou art the Christ, the son of the living God.*" So we have these two, a man and a woman, who experienced this central revelation of the gospels.

What we learn in the story told by John is that Martha was active in all aspects of life, not just cleaning house and cooking for guests. She got things done. She might even have been a little forward and demanding –one who pushed other people to accomplish. But—and this is important—the thing that drove her was a foundational faith and testimony that her friend and Lord was indeed the Christ.

Mary's personality was much more passive and quiet, but it was she who empathized with the needs of Christ before the crucifixion and poured the bottle of perfume over his head. She was not passive in that act but was willing to incur the wrath of the practical men standing about watching her. By this act of caring love, she gave a ministry that was desperately needed and which others had not been sensitive enough to give.

> What we discover in these accounts of Mary and Martha is that the contemplative and active need not be separated but can exist in the same person. Even those who take care of the practical affairs of the world can give the most significant testimony of all, "*Thou art the Christ, the Son of the living God.*" And the quiet, more studious and thoughtful people can, when the occasion demands, perform the courageous act of love. When Christ, as Luke tells the story, said, "*But one thing is needful and Mary has chosen that good part which shall not be taken away from her,"* he was both commending Mary and stating a basic principle: the one thing needful, regardless of what we do, is to have a foundation of faith and a life centered in him. We are to set our hearts on him and then act in whatever capacity he calls us.
>
> Velma Ruch, *Signature of God,* 465-467.

**PRAYER:** Dear Universal God, we are so grateful that diversity in temperament, culture, and race is pleasing to you. You have created every aspect of the universe to show the great variety of which your creative power is capable. Help us to understand more clearly the joy of such richness and make our personal expression of who we are a witness of your love for us. Amen.

# THE SIXTH TUESDAY OF EASTER: JOHN, THE DISCIPLE JESUS LOVED

**Repentance:**
**The weight of past and fruitless guilt**
**God wills to lighten by his grace.**
**Deep prayer, persistent faith unite**
**His great compassion to embrace.**
Cleo Hanthorne Moon, *Hymns of the Saints,* No.118.

**SCRIPTURE:** **Luke 9:51-56 "Send Down Fire":**
*When the days drew near for him to be taken up, he set his face to go to Jerusalem. And he sent messengers ahead of him. On their way they entered a village of the Samaritans to make ready for him; but they did not receive him, because his face was set toward Jerusalem. When his disciples James and John saw it, they said, "Lord, do you want us to command fire to come down from heaven and consume them?" But he turned and rebuked them. Then they went on to another village.*

**MEDITATION: Growth in Christ**

John may have been little more than a teenager when he decided to follow Jesus. If he truly is the author of the Gospel of John he probably was close to one hundred years old when it was written and compiled. What a remarkable growth in the span of that lifetime! From some of the early stories about him, he and his brother obviously made a name for themselves by their enthusiastic and somewhat brash actions. John Killinger has written about them,

> Call down fire out of heaven. It was the sort of thing young disciples might want to do. Scuttle the ship, block the pass, blow up the ungrateful so-and-sos! And therefore says Mark, Jesus nicknamed James and John "Boanerges" – "sons of thunder." It is a good nickname, chosen with a sense of humor. Thunder, not lightning noisy but empty. Agitation and commotion.- movement without progress.
>
> It is often descriptive of the first season of ministry, when enthusiasm is still running high and disappointments have not tempered the imagination. Now, of course, it would be sons and daughters of thunder – those who are full of fury at the world because it has only the sense of a backward-walking duck and has not surrendered itself to the Master. Sons and daughters of commotion, who hope to bring in the kingdom with programs and marches and boycotts. ...
>
> One thing is sure: we know, when we get older, that we won't change the world the way we thought we would when we were young. ...Even the beloved disciple learned this, and from being a son of agitation or commotion became (we think) the author of a Gospel of love and confidence in the power of God to complete the work God has begun in Jesus Christ. We picture John at the end as placid and undisturbed, his

eyes resting calmly on a future that works itself out without the feverish and spasmodic assistance of the young Turks who think it will arrive tomorrow.

It just may be that we are not called to change everything in the world but to love it; and, in loving, it may change.

John Killinger, *Christ in the Seasons of Ministry,* 23-24, 34; used with permission

**"Love One Another"**

After John spent much time with Jesus on earth and many years as a leader of the early Church, with many issues to address in instructing the early Christians, his message became only more basic, "Love one another," he pleaded over and over. He had come to understand the essence of Jesus and of God the Father. He understood why Jesus came, why he died and rose, and why he promised a fantastic future for his own. Jesus possesses a love like no other, a love that only God can supply, and those who know Jesus can do nothing else but reflect that same love. Truly, the gospel message remains this simple: love God, and love your neighbor as yourself (Matthew 22:37-40).

What brought about such transformation in John? Jesus' death and resurrection moved like thunder in John's spirit, changing his aggression and pride to a love for Christ and others. John was transformed through the power of the resurrected Christ, and as he grew old his yearning to point to Jesus only increased.

*The Renovare Spiritual Formation Bible,* 2241; used with permission

**PRAYER:** O God, who loves us all, we thank you for your beloved servant John. Because of the imprint of your Spirit upon him he became one of the great witnesses of your love. He it was who told us "God is love" and ever since we have tried to encompass that truth in our hearts and minds. We thank you that the Christ that walked with John and the rest on the dusty roads of Galilee is still with us with his Spirit. May that presence burn itself into our hearts never to be forgotten. Amen.

# THE SIXTH WEDNESDAY OF EASTER: PETER IN PROCESS

**Promises to Keep:**
**O Jesus, I have promised To serve thee to the end;**
**Be thou forever near me, My Master and my Friend;**
**I shall not fear the battle If thou art by my side,**
**Nor wander from the pathway If thou wilt be my Guide.**
John E. Bode, *Hymns of the Saints,* No. 463

**SCRIPTURE:** **Luke 22:31-34 The Cock Will Not Crow …**

*"Simon, Simon, listen! Satan has demanded to sift all of you like wheat, but I have prayed for you that your own faith may not fail; and you, when once you have turned back, strengthen your brothers." And he said to him, "Lord, I am ready to go with you to prison and to death!" Jesus said, "I tell you, Peter, the cock will not crow this day, until you have denied three times that you know me."*

**Luke 22: 54-62. This Man Also Was with Him**

*Then they seized [Jesus] and led him away, bringing him into the high priest's house. But Peter was following at a distance. When they had kindled a fire in the middle of the courtyard and sat down together, Peter sat among them. Then a servant-girl, seeing him in the firelight, stared at him and said,. "this man also was with him." But he denied it, saying, "Woman, I do not know him." A little later someone else, on seeing him, said, "You also are one of them." But Peter said, "Man, I am not!" Then about an hour later still another kept insisting, "Surely this man also was with him, for he is a Galilean." But Peter said, "Man, I do not know what you are talking about!" At that moment, while he was still speaking, the cock crowed. The Lord turned and looked at Peter. Then Peter remembered the word of the Lord, how he had said to him, "Before the cock crows today, you will deny me three times." And he went out and wept bitterly.*

**MEDITATION: Peter's Dark Night of the Soul**

[When Jesus was seized and taken away] only two of the disciples dared to backtrack and trail Jesus as he was being led away. One was John, the disciple Jesus loved; the other, Peter.

Peter – the Gibraltar among the disciples. Tonight he would be reduced to a mere pebble of a man.

He would start the evening in a resolute posture in the upper room, "Lord, I am ready to go with you to prison and to death. Even if all fall away on account of you, I will never fall away." Later in the night he would stand single-handedly against a mob of Roman soldiers, wielding his sword in the torch-lit garden of Gethsemane. But before dawn, he wouldn't even be able to stand up to the stares of a young servant girl.

What could account for so great a defection from so dedicated a disciple?

The answer is carefully wrapped in words both plaintive and tender, "Simon, Simon. Satan has asked to sift you as wheat." …Tonight, into those hands Peter would fall. …

The hour is late; the night, dark and chilly. Peter has followed Jesus all the way to the temple courtyard where the Savior, under heavy guard, awaits his hearing. He comes because Jesus is his Lord, because Jesus would have come for him had the tables been turned. He comes to help, not knowing what he can do, or how, or when. A thousand scenarios crowd his mind. He is confused and torn: *Do I grab a sword and fight? No, he rebuked me for that in the garden. Do I testify on his behalf? A lot of good that would do. Do I just watch and listen so I can rally the disciples in the morning?*

Cloaked in anonymity, Peter comes to warm himself by a campfire, a radius of warmth shared by his Lord's captors. He comes to think, to sort things out, to plan his next move.

He sits, pushing his palms against the heat, rubbing his arms. He takes from the fire its warmth and the idle companionship of strangers small-talking the evening away...

"This man was with him"

Sometime later there is another accusation. And immediately another denial, only more forceful this time. Finally, his accent gives him away.

He would have to think quick to get around that one. He then curses and swears, letting loose a herd of expletives in hopes of kicking up enough dust to cloud his identity.

In no uncertain terms he denies any association with Jesus. The ploy seems to have worked. The circle wound around the campfire appears satisfied.

But somewhere in the night a rooster stretched its neck, shakes its feathers, and crows an indictment.

The disciple jerks his head around and catches Jesus looking at him. It is a brief moment, almost too short to be intimate. But a moment like this has a way of stretching and framing itself to hang in the mind ...

With that look, all of Peter's pent-up emotions suddenly cave in on themselves. He runs from the courtyard, bitter tears stinging his eyes. He stops somewhere outside and beats his fists against his chest. He pulls at his hair. He gnarls his face. The weight of his guilt is too much to bear. He collapses in a wailing heap.

He weeps for the Savior he has so miserably failed. And he weeps for himself. O God, *no, no, no. What have I done? God, take this one dark hour from me. Turn back the night. Give me another chance. Please, O God. Turn back the night.*

But the night will not be turned back. And this darkest of hours will not be taken from him.

When the tears finally do stop, the night has paled to gray. Soon it will be dawn.

The winnowing is over. All that is left is the naked kernel of faith. It is a small grain, but a grain Satan couldn't touch. He could winnow all the chaff he wanted, but the wheat belongs to Jesus.

Peter is a smaller man now without the thick husk that once surrounded his life. He is broken and he is bare.

Be hard on him if you like ...Go ahead. But before you do, remember that the other disciples had already deserted Jesus. Peter and John alone followed him that terrifying night.

True. Peter followed him at a distance. But still he followed...And it's true, he failed Jesus. But he failed in a courtyard where the others dared not set foot. And he failed not under normal pressure, but under the heavy winnow of Satan.

So go ahead. Be hard on him. But remember, it was Satan, not Jesus, who did the sifting.

Jesus was the one who prayed. (97-102).

Within seven weeks, Peter would preach the boldest sermon of his life. It would be in Jerusalem, the very bastion of hatred against Jesus. Three thousand would be saved. They would form the nucleus of the church he would establish there. Later, he would stand up to them in a bold confession for his Savior. And he would go on preaching about his crucified Lord, shaking the foundations of the temple and sending a tremor to rock even the mighty pillars of the Roman Empire ...

What kind of friend inspires devotion like that?

A friend who prayed for him when he was weak. A friend who forgave him when he failed. A friend who healed a painful memory. A friend who loved him. A friend who believed in him.

A friend like Jesus.

A friend who first laid down his life for him. (141-142)

Excerpts from Ken Gire, "An Intimate Moment with Peter," *Intimate Moments with the Savior* (Grand Rapids, Michigan: Zondervan,1989), 97-102, 141-142; used with permission

**PRAYER:** God of the weak and of the strong, we receive much encouragement from your servant, Peter. He was lovable, impulsive, made mistakes, but was never afraid to pick up the pieces and start again. You, who always see the good in us and see us as we can be, not necessarily as we are, accept our offerings to you even when they are sometimes flawed. We wish to rise to the heights of which we are capable with your help and become a blessing, as was Peter, to your people. Be our guide and strength, we pray. Amen.

# THE SIXTH THURSDAY OF EASTER
# ASCENSION DAY

The Ever-Present Christ: Not only is the presence of God in Jesus Christ to be experienced occasionally, the indwelling Christ is to become the shaping power of our lives. This is the dynamic of our spiritual formation.

Maxie Dunnam, *Alive in Christ*

**SCRIPTURE:** **Acts 1:3-11 "Is This the Time?"**

*After his suffering he presented himself alive to them by many convincing proofs, appearing to them during forty days and speaking about the kingdom of God. While staying with them, he ordered them not to leave Jerusalem, but to wait there for the promise of the Father "This," he said "is what you have heard from me; for John baptized with water, but you will be baptized with the Holy Spirit not many days from now."*

*So when they had come together, they asked him, "Lord, is this the time when you will restore the kingdom to Israel?" He replied, "It is not for you to know the times or periods that the Father has set by his own authority. But you will receive power when the Holy Spirit has come upon you; and you will be my witnesses in Jerusalem in all Judea and Samaria, and to the ends of the earth." When he had said this, as they were watching he was lifted up and cloud took him out of their sight.*

**MEDITATION: The Resurrected Jesus**

Jesus remained on earth for forty days. He gathered the disciples, who had fled in all directions when he was arrested and crucified. They were disheartened and lost, grieving their Master's death, certain the cause was lost, ashamed of their abandonment of him, fearful for their own lives. He appeared to them where they were, in ones and twos and small groups, and drew them back together. He shaped them into a community of believers, He continued his teaching urgently so because these first disciples were to be his witnesses to the world. They were to spread the Gospel, the Good News, not merely through Galilee and Judea, not merely among the Jews but throughout the whole world, to all peoples.

After he told the disciples all that they would one day do in his name and reassured them again that he would not abandon them but would send them the Advocate, He instructed them to remain together in Jerusalem "until you have been clothed with power from on high" (Luke 24:49). They were to do nothing, only wait and pray. And for ten days they waited. They stayed together. They prayed together. Only that. They didn't go out among the people. They made no plans for the future. They simply waited on the Spirit. Jesus' promise to them was fulfilled on the day we refer to as Pentecost.

Cindy Mortus

**How Beautiful the Feet**

At the liturgical moment of the ascension we observe the time during which the feet of Jesus last made intimate contact with the earth. This Jesus was God very much with us, feet firmly planted on the ground. Now a new relationship between God and the earth-home we inhabit begins. As Spirit, God would enter the community of believers and inspire them to take up the journey to be the feet that bring good news, the teachers at whose feet disciples sit, the foot-washers and those whose feet are washed, the feet that dance upon the grave.

Wendy Wright, *The Rising*, 164

**PRAYER:**

He lives in us! Immortal King! Creation bows to Him.
He breathed in us the breath of life To make us one with Him.

He lives for us! What joy is ours! He lightens every mind.
He quickens us to know our worth; We sense His grand design.

He lives through us! How great our task! What promise we fulfill!
Obedient to His spirit's call, We implement His will.

Linda E. Coffman *Hymns of the Saints,* No. 199

# THE SIXTH FRIDAY OF EASTER: THE TEN-DAY WAIT

**Patience:**

*It will be said on that day, Lo, this is our God; we have waited for him, so that he might save us. This is the Lord for whom we have waited; let us be glad and rejoice in his salvation*

(Isaiah 25:9).

**SCRIPTURE:** **Luke 24: 49, 52 Wait for Power from on High**

*"And see, I am sending upon you what my Father promised; so stay here in the city until you have been clothed with power from on high."*
*And they worshiped him, and returned to Jerusalem with great joy; and they were continually in the temple blessing God.*

**MEDITATION: Waiting**

Jesus asked the disciples to wait in Jerusalem until they received the promised power to meet all that lay ahead of them as well as an advocate to teach them all that they needed to know. It must have been hard to wait. They were under suspicion by the authorities; they wanted to get on with their lives; and how did they know that waiting would make any difference? The disciples were obedient to the command of Jesus, though, and their obedience was rewarded with power and with a companion.

> That power and that companion have been with us ever since. We claim the power of the Holy Spirit today to strengthen us for living fully, faithfully, and joyfully. We claim the companionship of Christ to guide, instruct, and sustain us day by day. Sometimes we wait for that power to become active or for that kind of companionship to blossom in our relationship with God in Christ. As we learn to earnestly seek and patiently wait – in God's perfect timing – the gifts are given. Then we know it was worth the wait.
>
> Rueben P. Job, *A Guide to Prayer for All Who Seek God* (Nashville: Upper Room Books, 2003), 212

Why was it important that the disciples waited? Why is it important for us to wait sometimes? It isn't waiting just for the sake of waiting that is important. Doing so may cultivate patience, but it will more likely lead to frustration and inactivity. What is critical is not that the disciples waited, but why the disciples waited. They trusted Jesus, their Lord, their Teacher, and their Beloved Friend, enough to do what he told them. They were obedient despite the struggles they faced – persecution and fear. Can you imagine what it must have felt like to be left again with only the memories and a promise that the Spirit would come by this One whom they loved more than anything, anyone? The disciples teach us something else in how they waited. The Gospel of Luke says that in their waiting they praised God and worshiped him.

> In this obedient waiting, when we wait as response to our best understanding of God's will we open ourselves to receive many gifts that we can share with others. In obedient waiting there is humility and surrender. We affirm that we are willing to live joyfully in God's time.
>
> Tacy Holliday

Reflect on a time in your own life when you waited in faith. What did you gain by waiting that helped you in future challenges?

**PRAYER:** *O Lord, we wait for you; your name and your renown*
*are the soul's desire.*
*My soul yearns for you in the night, my spirit within me*
*earnestly seeks you*
*O Lord, you will ordain peace for us, for indeed all we have*
*done you have done for us.*
*O Lord, our God, other lords besides you have ruled over us,*
*but we acknowledge your name alone. Amen.*

Isaiah 26: 8, 9, 12, 13

# THE SIXTH SATURDAY OF EASTER: THE MISSION TO BE

**Confidence in God's Promises:**

*Such is the confidence that we have through Christ toward God. Not that we are competent of ourselves to claim anything as coming from us; our competence is from God, who has made us competent to be ministers of a new covenant, not of letter but of spirit; for the letter kills, but the Spirit gives life*

(2 Corinthians 3:4-6).

**SCRIPTURE:** **Acts 1:6-8 The Call to Mission:**

*So when they had come together, they asked him, "Lord, is this the time when you will restore the kingdom to Israel?" He replied, "It is not for you to know the times* or *periods that the Father has set by his own authority. But you will receive power when the Holy Spirit has come upon you; and you will be my witnesses in Jerusalem, in all Judea and Samaria, and to the ends of the earth."*

**Mark 28:18-20 All Nations Are Included**

*And Jesus came and said to them, "All authority in heaven and on earth has been given to me. Go therefore and make disciples of all nations, baptizing them in the name of the Father and of the Son and of the Holy Spirit, and teaching them to obey everything that I have commanded you. And remember, I am with you always, to the end of the age.*

**MEDITATION: The Book of Acts and the Mission to Be**

One of Luke's aims [in the writing of the Book of Acts] was to show that Christianity was for all men of every country. This was one of the things that Jews found hard to grasp. They had the idea that they were God's chosen people and that God had no use for any other nation. Luke sets out to prove otherwise. He shows Philip preaching to the Samaritans; he shows Stephen making Christianity universal and being killed for it; he shows Peter accepting Cornelius into the Church; he shows the Christians preaching to the Gentiles at Antioch; he shows Paul traveling far and wide winning men of all kinds for Christ; and in Acts 15 he shows the Church making the great decision to accept the Gentiles on equal terms with the Jews.

But these were merely secondary aims. Luke's chief purpose is set out in the words of the Risen Christ in 1:8 "*You shall be my witnesses in Jerusalem and in all Judea and Samaria and to the end of the earth.*" It was to show the expansion of Christianity, and how that religion which began in a little corner of Palestine had in not much more than thirty years reached Rome.

Throughout his ministry Jesus labored under one great disadvantage. The center of his message was the kingdom of God (Mark 1:14); but he meant one thing by the kingdom and those who listened to him meant another.

The Jews were always vividly conscious of being God's chosen people [They looked] forward to a day when God would break directly into human history and establish that world sovereignty of which they dreamed. They conceived of the kingdom in political terms.

How did Jesus conceive of it? Let us look at the Lord's Prayer. In it there are two petitions side by side. "*Thy kingdom come; they will be done in earth as it is in heaven*" .Therefore, we see that by the kingdom Jesus meant a society upon earth where God's will would be as perfectly done as it is in heaven. Because of that it would be a kingdom founded on love and not on power.

To attain that, men needed the Holy Spirit…We are not to think that the Spirit came into existence now for the first time. It is quite possible for a power always to exist but for men to experience or take it at some given moment …So God is eternally Father, Son and Holy Spirit, but there came to men a special time when they experienced to the full that power which had always been present.

> The power of the spirit was going to make them Christ's witnesses. That witness was to operate in an ever-extending series of concentric circles, first in Jerusalem, then throughout Judea; then Samaria, the semi-Jewish state, would be a kind of bridge leading out into the heathen world; and finally this witness was to go out to the ends of the earth.
>
> William Barclay, *The Acts of the Apostles,*
> (Westminster John Knox Press, 1976), 4-12

Two thousand years have passed since the Book of Acts was written. What Luke is bringing us in that story is as challenging to us today as it was twenty centuries ago.

We are still trying to conceive how to put into practice those immortal words of Jesus: *"Thy kingdom come; they will be done on earth as it is in heaven."* The Restoration movement called the dream Zion and challenged each of us to make the places we occupy to "*shine as Zion, the redeemed of the Lord.*" How are we doing? Meditate on your own contribution to the cause of Zion.

**PRAYER:** So often God, we leave the difficult challenges that face us to some one else to carry out. We often fail to recognize in our global village that we carry responsibility for the welfare of persons way beyond our immediate family and community. We confess our sin before you and pray that the Spirit that descended on those early Christians will descend on us to give us eyes to see and ears to hear the cries of those in need. Strengthen our will to serve and fill our hearts with compassion for those whose sufferings we can help relieve, we pray. Amen.

# THE SEVENTH WEEK OF EASTER INSPIRED BY THE LIFE AND WITNESS OF THE REDEEMER OF THE WORLD

Our life of discipleship calls us to be deeply involved in three areas; our individual communion with God; our participation in the community of the church, the body of Christ; and our outreach in mission to the larger world community. The Temple so effectively symbolizes all three: the Worshipers' Path where we commune with God in a one on One situation; the sanctuary where individually prepared we move in to be part of the body of Christ; the sending forth to be messengers of the life and witness of the Redeemer of the world. The principles by which this can be accomplished are stated in Section 156 of the Doctrine and Covenants and serve as focus points for this week's meditations.

---

## THE SEVENTH SUNDAY OF EASTER: SPIRITUAL AWAKENING

**Awakening:**

*"Sleeper awake! Rise from the dead, and Christ will shine on you."*
(Ephesians 5:14).

**SCRIPTURE:** **Doctrine and Covenants, 156:3 Ministries Yet to Come**

*My servants have been diligent in the work of planning for the building of my temple in the Center Place. Let this work continue at an accelerated rate, according to the instructions already given; for there is great need of the spiritual awakening that will be engendered by the ministries experienced within its walls.*

**Doctrine and Covenants, 157:8 A Shining Symbol**

*I, the Lord, am well pleased with the progress of your preparations toward the building of my temple in the Center Place. Those who have prepared themselves bytraining and education to assist, whether within the body or otherwise, will be blessed according to their need insofar as they seek me and call on my name. If they will thus open themselves, then I will pour out my Spirit on all the laborers together, to the end that a shining symbol of my love and my desires for my creation my rise in beauty before the world.*

**Doctrine and Covenants, 161:2 a,b Becoming a People of the Temple**

Become a people of the Temple – those who see violence but proclaim peace, who feel conflict yet extend the hand of reconciliation, who encounter broken spirits and find pathways for healing. Fulfill the purposes of the Temple by making its ministriesmanifest in your hearts.

**MEDITATION: Spiritual Awakening**

Saints, it *is* time for a spiritual awakening. I do not need to remind anyone of the secular emptiness awaiting the maturation of our finest and brightest children and grandchildren. I do not need to tell of parents who agonize over delightful youth caught in deadening life-styles which rob them of productive futures. Many of us know the agony of struggling congregations where hostility destroys unity, breeds mistrust, and denies the faith once delivered to our parents, grandparents, and other spiritual giants of the past. And we all know of homes broken by selfish sensuality or flippant unwillingness to assume responsibility for "what God hath joined together." These people are not strangers in some far-off place. They are in our families, our congregations, our communities. The world is piled high with problems. They are problems we face as individuals, as families, as congregations, as a church, and as nations in a global community. The world around us and we as individuals are weak, uncertain, and unstable. This awareness presents us with a sense of urgency in our call for spiritual awakening. We need it personally. We need it as a church. And the nations we represent need to be impacted by the life and message of the Prince of Peace.

Paul Booth in sermon given at the 1986 World Conference;
published in the *Saints Herald* (June 1986): 12-14, 16

What does "spiritual awakening" mean to you? How would you describe it?. Has it happened to you? If so, how? What do you believe was the import of the statement in Section 156, "There is great need for the spiritual awakening that will be engendered by ministries experienced within its [the temple] walls"?

**Learning from Others**

The nature, disposition, and experience of individuals determine to some extent the means by which each may be touched by the higher revelation. For the mystics, as delineated in "the mystic way," awakening is our first conscious apprehension of the Infinite. It is a realization that the universe is sacramental and that there is a Greater Life surrounding and sustaining our own. The experience may be a sudden and dramatic one, as in the case of Saul of Tarsus, or it may be so gradual that we have no remembrance of when first we knew. Some of us, I believe, are born with this knowledge. The experience must, however, be existential and firsthand, not the mere repetition of what we learned at home or at church school. These teachings may indeed prepare us for the moment of awakening just as conscientious study and intellectual apprehension of a given subject may one day be transformed so that suddenly we existentially understand what we may have intellectually accepted for a long time. Following the voice in the whirlwind, Job had an experience of awakening when he exclaimed in wonder, "*I have heard of Thee by the hearing of the ear, but now mine eye seeth Thee.*" Something similar happened to Jesus' disciples. It was one thing to know Jesus the man, quite another for them to be able to say with Peter, "*Thou art the Christ, the Son of the Living God.*"

Awakening is a conversion experience – not to specific theological beliefs but to a recognition of the presence and power of the Infinite.

For many it is an experience similar to awakening after having slept. For some who have considered themselves religious and then discover the reality of what they have believed, it is, says one writer, "a change of taste – the most momentous one that ever occurs in human experience." The experience is always perceived as a gift. The individual recognizes that at some point time and eternity touched and life was no longer the same. The question always arises, How does it happen? Is there any way to personally prepare for the experience or even to assist others on the way? Yes, of course, it can be prepared for. A deep-seated desire and a change of self make a difference. I also believe that while one's family and friends may not be able to give the gift directly, they can be "God bearers" and nurture the mystic faculty which in its incipient stage is available to all. Jung in his elaboration of the collective unconscious suggested that as individuals we participate in both physical and spiritual inheritance. A developed spiritual life in parents can be transmitted to their children. It does make a difference not only with what spirit the child is born but also with what type of commitment children are surrounded as they grow. In the giving of the gift, parents become co-creators with God. The gift may be part of but different from stories about Jesus. It is atmosphere; it is unspoken; it is presence by spirit, not by words. Indirectly, parents help to lay for their children the foundations of joy. They have no greater gift to give. It is thus that for many awakening may occur even before birth and through nurture become an abiding presence. Over a lifetime we grow in our understanding of what that Presence signifies.

Velma Ruch, *The Signature of God,* 327-333

**PRAYER:** **O Christ, my Lord, create in me,**
The person I am meant to be.
My soul estranged, I'm prone to sin;
Redeem my life, without, within.

O Lord, may every soul embrace
The wonders of your matchless grace.
From guilt and fear each one set free;
Create a new humanity.

O Christ, make visible your Church,
As all for life and meaning search.
Your will be done! O set aflame
That fellowship which bears your name.

Emmanuel, O Prince of Peace,
To every nation bring release.
Beat from each sword a plowshare strong;
Your kingdom come: my prayer, my song. Amen.

Chester E. Custer, *Hymns of the Saints,* No. 174

# THE SEVENETH MONDAY OF EASTER: THE PURSUIT OF PEACE

**Share the Peace:**

We begin to experience the peace of Jesus Christ as we are being reconciled to God, to others, to ourselves, and to creation. This is the heart of the gospel as we are called to live it and proclaim it
(Steve Veazey, Inaugural Sermon, 2005 World Conference).

**SCRIPTURE:** **Doctrine and Covenants 156:5a Peace**

*The temple shall be dedicated to the pursuit of peace. It shall be for reconciliation and for healing of the spirit.*

**MEDITATION: The Temple**

The Temple is not only a place, but is also a symbol of who and what the church is to be. We know the church is not defined as a collection of buildings, but as a community of people. In this sense, the Temple is to symbolize the communal formation for us as a people.

> The Spirit says that the Temple is dedicated to a "pursuit." This implies seeking, movement, direction, action response. Pursuit occurs through the intentionality of our life. It is a choice and decision to respond and move. The pursuit for peace, reconciliation, healing of the spirit seem to be descriptors that define our desire for seeking wholeness.
>
> Scott Murphy

**The Challenge Before Us**

My friends, we have an enormous and wonderful challenge before us. Our [Community of Christ] Christian witness compels us to speak peace, justice, and compassion to a world in desperate need. Our scriptures do not provide us with even a definition or set of specific instructions. What we do have is the story of how one person and his followers pursued peace in their day and time, a time so unlike our own that only the principles are relevant for us and our world …

What we must seek is the living word of God for today, which in our best moments the Community of Christ has always done, which word will have the power to move, change, and inspire us. The task is enormous and we are a small church, but we do not act alone. People of spiritual goodwill all over the world are responding to the imperative for peace in unprecedented numbers and in unprecedented ways. Their efforts are beginning to make a difference.

Most important, we do not act alone because the Spirit of God precedes us and shows us the way if we have eyes to see. Do we dare believe that it is the pursuit of peace that can have the unifying power to bring together people of good will, wherever they dwell, whatever language they speak, and whatever or whomever they call God? May we resolve to do the work of peace to those places where we serve, and in the words of Captain Kirk [of Star Trek] "to boldly go where no [one] has gone before"?

Barbara M. Higdon, "A Time of True Shalom," *Shepherds Abiding in the Field,* Leonard Young, ed. (Herald House: 1997), 217-218

**PRAYER:** **A Daily Prayer for Peace**

We thank you, praise you.

You are the fountain of the living water, light in the dark. There is peace when we are with you. There are sorrows and burdens, but if we listen to you, look up to you, come close to you, then we will have happiness and joy. Our souls will be revived. In this world still full of confusion, we sincerely ask. May the Lord, our source of peace, give this world peace at all times and in every way. We rely on you firmly to keep us in perfect peace. In you nothing is impossible. Your surprising peace will fill everyone's heart, no matter who they are or from which country.

May the glory be yours for ever and ever. In this way I pray in Jesus' name. Amen.

Mickael Tzeng, Taiwan, September 7, 1999

# THE SEVENTH TUESDAY OF EASTER
# RECONCILIATION AND HEALING OF THE SPIRIT

**Transformation:**

Earth, isn't this what you want
An invisible rearising in us;
What is your urgent command
If not transformation?

Rilke

**SCRIPTURE:** **Doctrine and Covenants 156:5e The Life and Witness of the Redeemer of the World**

*And it shall be a place in which the essential meaning of the Restoration as healing and redeeming agent is given new life and understanding, inspired by the life and witness of the Redeemer of the world.*

**Doctrine and Covenants 157:15 Be Reconciled**

*Come and be reconciled in my body is the healing word to those who are saddened and downhearted.*

**2 Corinthians 5:17-20 A New Creation**

*So if anyone is in Christ, there is a new creation; everything old has passed away, see, everything has become new! All this is from God who reconciled us to himself through Jesus Christ, and has given us the ministry of reconciliation; that is in Christ God was reconciling the world to himself, not counting their trespasses against them, and entrusting the message of reconciliation to us. So we are ambassadors for Christ, since God is making his appeal through us.*

**MEDITATION: Reconciliation – The Discipline of Love**

The concern for reconciliation finds expression in the simple human desire to understand others and to be understood by others ...Everyone wants to be cared for, to be sustained by the assurance that [he/she] shares in the watchful and thoughtful attention of others. – not merely or necessarily others in general but others in particular ...When the need to be cared for is dishonored, threatened, or undermined, then the individual cannot experience his own self as a unity his life may become deeply fragmented and splintered ...

The talent of reconciliation may be native to the personality of [the one] who has it – I do not know. But I am confining my thoughts, to begin with, to the inner reconciliation that an individual experiences when he feels that his life is bottomed by another's caring ...There must be a discipline either to develop the talent or to keep it alive. And in what does such a discipline consist? In the first place, there must be the intent itself. The individual must want to do it. A climate must be generated out of which the talent or gift moves forth into the life of another ...The mood that induces trust has to be developed and projected, given to training in the direction of trust and confidence.

The discipline of reconciliation for the religious [person] cannot be separated from the discipline of religious experience. In religious experience a [person] has a sense of being touched at his inmost center, at his very core, and this awareness sets in motion the process that makes for integration, his wholeness ...The sins, bitterness, weakness, virtues, loves, and strengths are all gathered and transmuted by God's love and grace, and we become whole in his Presence. This is the miracle of religious experience – the sense of being totally dealt with, completely understood, and utterly cared for. This is what a [person] seeks with his fellows. This is why the way of reconciliation and the way of love finally are one way.

What then is the nature of the discipline that love provides? In the first place, it is something that I must quite deliberately want to do. For many of us this is the first great roadblock. In our relations with each other there is often so much that alienates, that is distasteful; there seems to be every ground for refraining from the kind of concern that love demands.

In the second place, I must find the opening or openings through which my love can flow into the life of the other, and at the same time locate in myself openings through which his love can flow into me. Most often this involves an increased understanding of the other person ...There must be both a spontaneous and a deliberate response to such knowledge which will result in the sharing of resources at their deepest level ...

The willingness to be to another human being what is needed at the time the need is most urgent and most acutely felt – this is to participate in a precise act of redemption. This is to stand for one intimate moment *in loco dei* in the life of another – that is, to make available to another what has already been given to us ...To the degree to which our imagination becomes the *angelos* [messenger] of God, we ourselves may become his *instruments.*

> In the third place, there must be a sense of leisure out of which we relate to others ...We cannot be in a hurry in matters of the heart ...Whatever we learn of leisure in the discipline of silence, in meditation and prayer, bears rich, ripe fruit in preparing the way for love ...How indescribably wonderful and healing it is to encounter another human being who listens not only to our words, but manages, somehow, to listen to us. Everyone needs this and everyone needs to give it, as well – thus we come full circle in love...The experience of love is either a necessity or a luxury. If it be a luxury, it is expendable; if it be a necessity, then to deny it is to perish. So simple is the reality and so terrifying.

Excerpts from Howard Thurman's chapter "Reconciliation" in his book *Disciplines of the Spirit* (Richmond, Indiana: Friends United Press, 1987, c.1963); used with permission

**The Disciplines of Discipleship**

Since the time of Paul and before, disciples of Christ have been entrusted with the message of reconciliation. For the Community of Christ the transforming goal is to "become a world-wide church dedicated to the pursuit of peace, reconciliation and healing of the spirit." That statement appearing in Section 156 has the possibility of transforming the church. It has to do with the consecration of a people. It was to remind us of exactly this that the Temple was built. The possibility of peace, individually and collectively is God's most precious gift to us. It is the same peace that Christ promised his disciples so long ago. "*Peace be with you,*" he said. "*As the Father has sent me, so send I you...Receive the Holy Spirit.*" In those words the intimate connection between peace and the presence of the Holy Spirit was affirmed. We recognize that we cannot be effective servants of Christ without a personal process of continuous transformation, the heroic practice of the disciplines of discipleship. "It costs," wrote T. S. Eliot, "not less than everything."

What must be our response to this task before us? It calls for a prayer life ever open to divine presence; for a spirituality that grants power in the midst of weakness; for rootage in our heritage and ability to re-create the gospel for a new world; for a developing competence in the gifts that are ours; for a recognition of what it means to magnify our calling; for a love that is centered in Christ and inclusive of all; for a shining humility that radiates faith, hope, love, joy, and peace.

This "presence" to which we are called will inevitably by its very nature lead us into new avenues of reconciliation and healing of the spirit. We may find ourselves standing on the frontier in our own homes in breaking new ground in our understanding of our spouse or our children or in gaining the insight and love that can lead to conflict resolution and the blessings of peace and joy. It may be in greater understanding of those with whom we work and quiet ministry in places of need. It may be in assuming a position that is highly visible or one in the background where the healing touch and the blessing of the Divine will not be one necessarily recognized by many people. It may be that the frontier is in our own lives as we are overcome by age or illness or the multitude of things that can weigh us down. In all of these, regardless of what age or position in which we find ourselves, the secret to joy and fulfillment is a practiced recognition of the presence of the Divine in our lives, an ability to listen and to hear that still, small voice of God as it speaks to us and ever leads us into the places God would have us occupy.

The great adventure to which we are called will mean new life styles, new ways of understanding, a difference in our work, in economics, in politics, in government. Most of all it will depend upon our ability to remain whole and radiant, carrying the presence of the Divine into every situation in which we find ourselves. What is your response to this challenge?

**PRAYER:**

Here we have come, dear Lord, to thee,
Of thy transforming grace aware.
We humbly ask that we thy love,
Thy work, they joy henceforth may share.

We bring to thee no glorious gift,
No gift that from our strength we've made.
Forgive us for the wasted years,
Afar from thee, alone, afraid.

Accept our true repentance, Lord.
All that we are, for thee we'll strive,
And beg thy dear forgiving grace
To touch our wasted gifts alive. Amen.

Cleo Hanthorne Moon, *Hymns of the Saints*, No.109

# SEVENTH WEDNESDAY OF EASTER: WHOLENESS OF BODY, MIND AND SPIRIT

**The Promise:**

*"I came that they might have life and have it more abundantly"*

(John 10:10).

**SCRIPTURE:** **Doctrine and Covenants 156:5c Wholeness**

*By its ministries an attitude of wholeness of body, mind, and spirit as a desirable end toward which to strive will be fostered.*

**Matthew 22:37-40 Love of God and Neighbor**

*"You shall love the Lord your God with all your heart, and with all your soul, and with all your mind. This is the greatest and first commandment. And a second is like it: You shall love your neighbor as yourself. On these two commandments hang all the law and the prophets."*

**MEDITATION: Healing: The Restoration of Wholeness**

The relationship between "heal" and "whole" is obvious, although we may overlook their intimate connection and forget that the purpose of healing is not a *cure* but rather the restoration of wholeness ...Before we can become whole, at whatever cost, we must recognize our brokenness as part of the human condition ...But there is a paradox. While brokenness is a presupposition of our humanity and while God is with us in our brokenness, the whole message of the gospel is that we are intended to be whole. We are missing the point if we read the healing stories as accounts of medical cures of specific ailments – ah, this is how Jesus deals with a malfunctioning optic nerve; this is how he controls bleeding of unknown origin without recourse to surgery; this is how he rehabilitates the paralyzed. Christ's mission of healing is a mission of the restoration of wholeness. In other words, the healed become the people God intended them to be: intact, complete, and functioning. They are in harmony with themselves, with others, and with God.

It is tempting to read gospel accounts of healing as "happily-ever-after" stories: the story ends with the restoration of health and wholeness. It is easy to forget that healing can be difficult, frightening, and challenging. When the beggar Bartimaeus asked to receive his sight, did he know how much his blindness had protected him from pain and ugliness, how it had shielded him from really knowing the world around him? Being healed restored him to full participation and accountability in the human family.

Sometimes it is hard for the healed to go home again ...Healing, after all, does not erase the slate. Out of our brokenness we can gain compassion and insight, and ugly scars and hurts can become the raw material for creating rich and beautiful texture. The people healed by Jesus did not go back and live their lives over, this time without blemish. Rather, their brokenness became the fruitful matrix for a new life of wholeness.

The God who keeps track of sparrows – and no doubt starlings and pigeons as well – most assuredly keeps track of those made in God's image. God cannot forget us, and God can indeed "re-member" us; put us back together again, restore us to wholeness.

From Margaret Guenther, *Toward Holy Ground*
(Boston: Couley Publications, 1995) 78-96

### Wholeness

Wallace B. Smith notes that our modern world often fragmentizes our lives. It isolates the physical world from the psychic world,

> Seeing reality as an unbroken whole has a venerable history reaching back to the ancient Egyptians and Greeks. Venturesome physicians now take a wholistic approach to medicine and define health as a condition of wholeness of body, mind, and spirit. Modern medicine increasingly recognizes that the mind and body are one psychosomatic whole. Emotions influence bodily health, and bodily conditions react upon the personality.
>
> "Wholeness – A Quality Life-style," *Saints Herald* (January 1979): 6

Conversion, centering our lives in Christ in order to achieve wholeness of being is not the miracle of the moment when we rise from the waters of baptism. The making of a disciple is the task of a lifetime and beyond. We commit ourselves to Christ in order to become new persons in him. What we are aiming for is what Paul called "fullness of being." In this journey we have the restorative power of God's grace. Without it, life will forever remain less than whole. Denis Duncan has said, "The integration of the human personality is, in my view, impossible without the activity of the Holy Spirit. This is fundamental to our view of the aims of life and their fulfillment through personality."

Jesus in praying for his disciples said, "*And this is eternal life, that they may know you, the only true God, and Jesus Christ whom you have sent*" (John 17:3). It is the testimony of many that this is the only way to fullness of being. Transformation, salvation, is impossible without it. Salvation is, after all, restoration to wholeness. "*All this is from God, who reconciled us to himself through Christ, and has given us the ministry of reconciliation; that is, in Christ God was reconciling the world to himself* (2 Corinthians 5:18-19).

**PRAYER:** Loving God, in our often confused and discordant lives we feel lost and incomplete. Help us to find our bearings in you as we strive to become rooted and grounded in love. We know our salvation is in you and want to overcome the barriers that keep us estranged from you and the fullness of being possible through you. Fill our hearts with your grace and love and guide us into the fullness of your presence. We pray in the name of the living Christ. Amen.

# THE SEVENTH THURSDAY OF EASTER: A STRENGTHENING OF FAITH AND WITNESS

**Invocation:**

My faith looks up to thee, Thou Lamb of Calvary,
Savior Divine! Now hear me while I pray,
Take all my guilt away;
Oh, let me from this day Be wholly thine!

Ray Palmer, *Hymns of the Saints,* No. 143

**SCRIPTURE:** **Doctrine and Covenants 156:5b Faith and Witness**

*It shall also be for a strengthening of faith and preparation for witness.*

**Hebrews 11; 12:1-2 Assurance of Things Hoped For**

*Now faith is the assurance of things hoped for, the conviction of things not seen. Indeed by faith our ancestors received approval. By faith we understand that the worlds were prepared by the word of God, so that what is seen was made from things that are not visible ...By faith Abel offered to God a more acceptable sacrifice than Cain's...By faith Abraham obeyed when he was called to set out for a place that he was to receive as an inheritance; and he set out, not knowing where he was going. ..By faith Moses, when he was grown up, refused to be called a son of Pharaoh's daughter, choosing rather to share ill treatment with the people of God than to enjoy the fleeting pleasures of sin. And what more should I say? For time would fail me to tell of Gideon, Barak, Samson, Jephthah, of David and Samuel and the prophets—who through faith conquered kingdoms, administered justice,obtained promises, shut the mouth of lions...Others were tortured, refusing to accept release, in order to obtain a better resurrection. Others suffered mocking and flogging, and even chains and imprisonment. They were stoned to death, they were sawn in two, they were killed by the sword. Yet all these, though they were commended for their faith, did not receive what was promised, since God had provided something better so that they would not, apart from us, be made perfect.*

*Therefore, since we are surrounded by so great a cloud of witnesses, let us also lay aside every weight and the sin that clings so closely, and let us run with perseverance the race that is set before us, looking to Jesus the pioneer and perfecter of our faith, who for the sake of the joy that was set before him endured the cross, disregarding the shame, and has taken his seat at the right hand of God.*

**MEDITATION: Planting the Seed of Faith**

*Now as I said concerning faith – that it was not a perfect knowledge – even so it is with my words. You cannot know of their surety at first to perfection, any more than faith is a perfect knowledge.*

*But, behold, if you will awake and arouse your faculties, even to an experiment upon my words, and exercise a particle of faith, even if ye can no more than desire to believe, let this desire work in you even until you believe in a manner that you can give place for a portion of my words.*

*Now we will compare the word to a seed. It you give place that a seed may be planted in your heart, behold, if it be a true seed, or a good seed, and if you do not cast it out by your unbelief that you will resist the Spirit of the Lord, behold, it will begin to swell within your breasts.*

*And when you feel these swelling motions, you will begin to say within yourselves, "It must be a good seed, or that the word is good, for it begins to enlarge my soul; it begins to enlighten my understanding; and it begins to be delicious to me.*

*...And, behold , as the tree begins to grow, you will say, 'Let us nourish it with great care, that it may get root, that it may grow up and bring forth fruit to us.' And if you nourish it with much care, it will get root, and grow up, and bring forth fruit ...*

*Then, my brethren, you shall reap the rewards of your faith, and your diligence and patience and long-suffering, waiting for the tree to bring forth fruit to you.*

Book of Mormon, Alma 16: 149-154, 164, 173

**Growing in the Spirit**

The scriptures and meditations with which we have been involved these many days have all been geared to our growth in the Spirit, a growth that is the very basis of our faith and the transformation possible for us. For me, the quoted portion of the sixteenth chapter of Alma has always served as a blueprint for growth in the spiritual life. We are invited to awaken and arouse our faculties and exercise a particle of faith. We do not need to have it all when we begin. What we need is desire, a hunger that is intense enough that we are willing to listen and experiment. Alma asks us to give space that the seed of faith may be planted within us. That seed we have called prevenient grace. That grace is available to all who pay attention and respond to the movements within our breasts. We can test its value by the transformation that begins to take place within us. It begins "*to enlarge our soul, enlighten our understanding, and become delicious to us.*" What better tests could we have? It blesses soul, mind and spirit.

All this is the first flush of conversion. The seed has been planted, it has sprouted, and it has been discovered to be good. But what next? The plant that has begun to grow must be watered, nourished and tended to. If that happens it will take root, grow up, and bring forth fruit. If it is neglected, it will begin to wither away and the fruit of the tree, which is sweet above all that is sweet, white above all that is white, and pure above all that is pure, will be lost.

Howard Thurman in *Disciplines of the Spirit* compares growth in spiritual matters to growth in nature. It is characteristic, he says, of all forms of life to seek access to a source of vitality. It is amazing to discover how roots of trees, for example, grow toward sources of moisture or other nutrients. Once the nutrients are there, once the conditions of growth are met, energy becomes available and growth is inevitable.

In one respect, as human beings we may be different from trees and other plants. We don't always gravitate to our source of nourishment. We have a choice. If we do, however, submit to the conditions of growth, we become energized and become, as Alma described it, like trees that yield fruits of eternal life. But how do we do that? The people who listened to Alma wondered the same thing. It all comes down to practicing the presence as Amulek described it in verses 219-222 of chapter 16:

*Humble yourselves, and continue in prayer to him; cry to him when you are in your fields and over all your flocks; cry to him in your houses, and over all your household, morning, midday,and evening; cry to him against the power of your enemies; cry to him against the devil, who is an enemy to all righteousness... but this is not all: you must pour out your souls in your closets and your secret places, and in your wilderness. And when you do not cry to the Lord, let your hearts be full, drawn out in prayer to him continually for your welfare and also for the welfare of those who are around you.*

All this is good, but it turns out we cannot stop there. Amulek goes on, "*Now, behold,... do not suppose that this is all; for after you have done all these things, if you turn away the needy and the naked, and visit not the sick and afflicted, and impart not of your substance if you have, to those who stand in need, behold, your prayer is vain and avails you nothing, and you are as hypocrites who deny the faith.*" Nourishing the spirit within, practicing the presence of the Lord, and moving out in witness and service are two sides of the same coin. We cannot truly have one without the other. That is why the exhortation to "Go tell!" is part of any genuine spiritual experience and why a strengthening of faith will always lead to witness in word and deed.

**PRAYER:** *For this reason I bow my knees before the Father, from whom every family in heaven and on earth takes its name. I pray that, according to the riches of his glory, he may grant that you may be strengthened in your inner being with power through his Spirit, and that Christ may dwell in your hearts through faith, as you are being rooted and grounded in love. I pray that you may have the power to comprehend, with all the saints, what is the breadth and length and height and depth, and to know the love of Christ that surpasses knowledge, so that you may be filled with all the fullness of God.*

*Now to him who by the power at work within us able to accomplish abundantly more than we can ask or imagine, to him be glory in the church and in Christ Jesus to all generations forever and ever. Amen*

(Ephesians 3:14-21).

# THE SEVENTH FRIDAY OF EASTER: BY STUDY AND BY FAITH

**SCRIPTURE:** **Doctrine and Covenants 156:5d Leadership Education**

*It shall be the means for providing leadership education for priesthood and member.*

**Doctrine and Covenants 9:3 a-d Oliver Cowdery**

*Behold, you have not understood; you have supposed that I would give it unto you, when you took no thought, save it was to ask of me; but, behold, I say unto you, that you must study it out in your mind; then you must ask me if it be right, and if it is right, I will cause that your bosom shall burn within you; therefore, you shall feel that it is right; but if it be not right, you shall have no such feelings, but you shall have a stupor of thought, that shall cause you to forget the thing that is wrong.*

**Doctrine and Covenants 85:21 b,e.**

*And I give unto you a commandment, that you shall teach one another the doctrine of the kingdom; teach ye diligently and my grace shall attend you, that you may be instructed more perfectly in theory, in principle, in doctrine, in the law of the gospel, in all things that pertain unto the kingdom of God, that is expedient for you to understand ...that ye may be prepared in all things when I shall send you again, to magnify the calling whereunto I have called you and the mission with which I have commissioned you.*

**MEDITATION:**

In recent years there has been much talk of theologians and seminary students who found it quite easy to divorce analytic thinking from the experiential reality of that which they were studying. Kierkegaard tells an amusing story about such a situation. He describes a scene at the Last Judgment when the Lord is confronted by a professor of theology. The Lord asks, "Did you seek first the kingdom of God?" The professor responds"

> No, that I cannot say. But 'seek first the kingdom of God,' that I know how to say in seven languages: in Danish, in German, in French, in Greek, in Hebrew, in Latin, in Arabic, in Aramaic, in Phoenician...But I notice that I know it in nine languages, two more than I promised." Our Lord turns his back on him while the professor goes on: "It is simply that I have put all my effort into investigation and research, day and night." It is here that the angel Gabriel interrupts him with a boot that knocks him for a million miles.
>
> Quoted in Jaques Colette, ed. *Kierkegaard: The Difficulty of Being Christian* (The University of Notre Dame Press, 1960), 181

Kierkegaard one other time said it even more simply. He referred to those "who think in a palace and live in a doghouse." What all this says is that we need to relate a technique of investigation to an account of being.

## Sacred Knowledge

I have two chapters in my book *The Signature of God* in which I deal with these issues. One is called, "Intelligence, the Glory of God." The other is "Sacramental Learning." The first chapter discusses sacred knowledge, not as a special branch of knowledge that involves some areas of study and blocks out others. It is the approach that differs. It is what is involved in the statement, "*Seek learning by study and by faith.*" Sacred knowledge utilizes all the powers of reason, both the acquired and the given, and is related to love and spiritual perfection. It is to suggest that true knowledge is not possible without love, virtue, light, and truth.

In the other chapter, "Sacramental Learning" I try to distill some of the educational philosophy that developed in me over forty years of teaching in a Christian college. "Sacramental Learning" is a recognition that all finite things reveal infinitude. It means to set our heart on the sacred and think.

In 1962 I participated in a Danforth Seminar held in California at Pacific School of Religion. The topic of the seminar was "The Development of Moral and Spiritual Values in the College." As part of that seminar I wrote a paper on the characteristics that should mark a Christian scholar. Below is an abbreviated summary of those principles because I believe they apply to all of us who conduct our study and teaching under the mantle of the Spirit of God.

## Christian Scholars: Guides in Christian Learning

**1.** A Christian scholar must have intellectual integrity and scholarly competence. As such scholars we must at all times subject ourselves to the discipline of our chosen subjects but with the awareness that the motivation for study is never simply the accumulation of knowledge for its own sake. It always has to be knowledge for the sake of God, for our widening appreciation of him, and for our particular responsibility to ourselves and the society of which we are a part.

**2.** In the search for truth, we, as Christian scholars must have minds and spirits able to initiate and sustain critical and disturbing inquiry. In order to do that we have to have a foundation on which to stand. Such a foundation gives us the existential trust that makes it possible for us to live in ambiguity, to recognize that we do not have all the answers and that at the very best we are only scratching the surface of reality. Alfred Tennyson wrote,

> Our little systems have their day,
> They have their day and cease to be.
> They are but broken lights of thee
> And thou, O Lord, art more than they.

Study as a spiritual discipline gives us courage to explore and liberates us from being boxed in in a limited view of reality.

**3.** As Christian scholars we must conduct our search with humility in regard to our capacity for knowing the truth, with an understanding of the imperfection of all human knowledge, but still with a firm conviction of the value of the human effort to know and a recognition of the power and strength that may come in the search.

**4.** As Christian scholars we must be committed. We are not allowed to play with ideas and enjoy them simply for their own sake. Ideas must co-inhere with the central commitment of our lives. Such commitment is neither narrow dogmatism nor an untested acceptance of cherished beliefs in a theological creed. The people of the world who have given important service, who have set others on fire, have never been neutral. They have been persons with great convictions at the center of their beings. The end of truth is never neutrality. Unless education teaches us to choose sides and, if need be, give our lives for un-neutral truth, it has failed in one of its major endeavors.

**5.** The Christian scholar should reflect the spirit of Christ. What we know can never be divorced from what we are. One does not discover truth and then live it. One lives so that the discovery of truth is possible. As Rufus Jones has said, "Truth is not just an intellectual apprehension, it is something you do. It is both a possession and a participation. You never stop satisfied with an intellectual apprehension of the object of search. You become what you seek."

**6.** For a Christian scholar study becomes part of our vocation. It is a call to partnership with the Divine and asks us to engage in a covenant relationship. At the base of such an experience is the certainty that God intends for all to move out of ignorance and darkness. We are partners with God in attempting to bring creative light and understanding to the world of which we are a part.

Dorothy Sayers said at one time that "It is the business of education to wait upon Pentecost." That is the moment when the intellect takes fire and we know to the very depth of our beings what before was only a mental exercise. The word becomes flesh and we see into the life of things. James Joyce referred to such an experience as "epiphany." Do you recall such experiences in your own life when you come to truly understand that which you have known for years? Can you relate to the listed characteristics of Christian scholars? Can you put them into practice in your own study?

**PRAYER:** O God of truth and wisdom, we are awed by the wonder of the universe in which we live and the love that caused you to send your Son to teach us how to have life and that abundantly. We are grateful for the knowledge beyond knowledge that allows us to be rooted and grounded in your love for us. :As we study to learn more of your way with us, may your Spirit enlighten our minds and hearts and lead us in the ways everlasting, we pray. Amen.

# THE SEVENTH SATURDAY OF EASTER: DEVOTION TO THE KINGDOM

**SCRIPTURE:** **Doctrine and Covenants 156:11b The Work of the Kingdom**

*Then, as you go forth to witness of my love and my concern for all persons, you will know the joy which comes from devoting yourselves completely to the work of the kingdom. To this end will my Spirit be with you. Amen.*

**Doctrine and Covenants 155:7-8. Workers in the Cause of Zion**

*Test my words. Trust in my promises for they have been given for your assurance and will bear you up in times of doubt ... The call is for workers in the cause of Zion; therefore neither tarry nor doubt that I am. I know your perplexities and I am aware of your uncertainties, but if you will call upon my name my Spirit will go before you into whatsoever place you are sent and I will continue to bless you as you have need.*

**MEDITATION: The Celebration of Witnessing to the Kingdom**

*You will know the joy that comes from devoting yourselves completely to the work of the kingdom.*

The discipline of witnessing is celebratory. At its heart is the joy of a life overflowing with the love of the Divine. The mark of the one that carries it is radiance, a radiance that cannot be contained but sheds its light abroad. Francis of Assisi is credited with saying, "Always preach Christ, use words when necessary." Words will indeed be necessary but they will mean very little unless they come from someone anointed with the joy of the gospel. "*You are God's own people,*" we read in 1 Peter 2:9, "*that you may declare the wonderful deeds of him who called you out of darkness into his marvelous light.*"

W. Paul Jones in an article in *Weavings* called "Joy and Religious Motivation" wrote:

> Joy is so precious that a person alive with delight glows. So it is with the church. Evanglism is gross salesmanship unless at the center of the church there are those whose lives themselves testify 'that neither death, nor life, nor angels, nor principalities, nor things present, not things to come, nor powers, nor height, nor depth, nor anything else in all creation will be able to separate us from the love of God in Christ Jesus our Lord,' It is sharing of a joy rendered visible by our joyousness. We are drawn toward faithfulness as shared joy – with one another and with the whole creation – by the intuition that union with God alone can satisfy our deepest yearning.
>
> *Weavings* (November/December 1993): 43; used with permission

Was it not this joy that caused the woman at the well, having found the source of living water, to run to town and proclaim the presence of the Messiah? She having once been in disrepute became as Helen Bruch Pearson called her, "a hauler of living water." Was not this what happened to the disciples when Jesus after the resurrection came through locked doors and said to them, "Peace be unto you. As the Father has sent me so send I you?" "And send them he did," writes Max Lucado:

Ports. Courtyards. Boats. Synagogues. Prisons. Palaces. They went everywhere. Their message of the Nazarene dominoed across the civilized world. They were an infectious fever. They were a moving organism. They refused to be stopped. Uneducated drifters who shook history like a house wife shakes a rug.

> My wouldn't it be great to see it happen again? Many sat it is impossible. The world is too hard. Too secular. Too post-Christian. This is the age of information , not regeneration. So we deadbolt the door for fear of the word … What would it take to light the fire again? Somehow, those fellows in the upper room did it. The did it without dragging their feet or making excuses. For them it was rather obvious, "All I know is that he was dead and now he is alive" (*No Wonder They Call Him Savior,* 163-164*).*
>
> Velma Ruch "The Discipline of Witnessing,"
> *The Order of Evangelists' Training Resource, 128-129*

**Zion: The Kingdom of God on Earth**

The concepts of Zion in the Restoration movement have gone through some revisions through the years, but always we have kept in focus the petition in the Lord's Prayer: "*Thy kingdom come. Thy will be done on earth, as it is in heaven.*" We recognize we have a responsibility to help bring about God's kingdom here on earth. Our focus is not primarily on a world to come but rather what we can accomplish for the welfare of humanity in this life. Our vision in this regard is becoming increasingly relevant in a time when people all over the world have been awakened to social injustice and the suffering of untold numbers of people.

> The challenge we face in regard to our vision of Zion is that we never forget that the transformation of human beings comes first. We cannot set out to transform the world unless we are transformed ourselves. The message must live in the messenger or the announcement is of little worth. When Jesus announced, "The Spirit of God is upon me," he was affirming that what the Spirit anointed him to speak already lived in him. He was the transmitter of what he himself lived. That was why he could say so confidently, "*Today the scripture has been fulfilled in your hearing*" (Luke 4:18-21). When we proclaim our message through spiritually vibrant lives, the message will be heard and lives will be transformed.
>
> Velma Ruch, *The Transforming Power of Prayer*, Vol. 2, 138-139

**PRAYER:** Lord, make us instruments of your peace;
Where there is hatred let your love increase.
Lord, make us instruments of your peace;
Walls of pride and prejudice shall cease,
when we are your instruments of peace,

Where there is hatred, we will sow your love;
Where there is injury, we will never judge.
Where there is striving, we will speak your peace;
To the people crying for release,

we will be you instruments of peace.
Where there is blindness, we will pray for sight;
Where there is darkness, we will shine our light.
Where there is sadness, we will bear their grief;
we will be your instruments of peace.

Kirk and Deby Dearman , *Sing a New Song,* No. 21

# PENTECOST/ENDOWMENT DAY THE SPIRIT CAME; THE CHURCH WAS FORMED

## SUNDAY, PENTECOST THE SPIRIT OF GOD LIKE A FIRE IS BURNING

**SCRIPTURE:** **Acts 2:1-13 Filled with the Holy Spirit**

*When the day of Pentecost had come, they were all together in one place. And suddenly from heaven there came a sound like the rush of a violent wind, and it filled the entire house where they were sitting. Divided tongues, as of fire, appeared among them, and a tongue rested on each of them. All of them were filled with the Holy Spirit and began to speak in other languages, as the Spirit gave them ability.*

**MEDITATION: Tongues of Flame**

Fire is a symbol used through the centuries by those who had no other way to express what they felt as the power of the Holy Spirit entered their being. Isaiah was touched with coals of fire from the altar of God. The fire in the bones of Jeremiah made it impossible for him to forsake his prophetic calling. The discouraged and despairing disciples on the road to Emmaus found the words of an unrecognized stranger caused their hearts to burn within them. Heart as used here is not referring to a part of our anatomy. For the Emmaus disciples and for us, heart means the totality of who we are with all our hopes, dreams, mistakes, and defeats. To have a burning heart is an attempt to describe what it is like when the Spirit mysteriously touches and transforms the very center of our being. The flame that burns within, perhaps even momentarily, partakes of the eternal and marks the rest of our lives.

**Fire!**

A powerful story outside of scripture comes from the seventeenth century scientist/philosopher Blaise Pascal. Pascal was perhaps one of the most brilliant persons who ever lived. Though he wrote in great confidence about the human relationship with the Divine, it was not until the night of November 23, 1654, when for two hours he had an experience of transcendent lucidity which became for him "immediate testimony of the meeting of a human order of facts and an order of transcendent truth" (J. H. Broome, *Pascal* [New York: Barnes and Noble, 1965], 225). The almost incoherent yet beautifully communicative statements which this master of French prose jotted down on a piece of parchment found sewn into his clothing after his death has become one of the major documents testifying to the powerful interaction possible between human and Spirit. Pascal begins with a simple word: FIRE. The God he experienced that night was not the God of "philosophers and scholars" but the "God of Abraham, God of Isaac, God of Jacob" who had communicated with and been instrumental in the lives of his servants. Pascal recognized both the greatness of the human soul and the despair of those who have forgotten the source of their being. The scriptural affirmation, "*And this is life eternal, that they might know thee, the only true God and Jesus Christ, whom thou has sent,*" he now knew existentially. Amidst "tears of joy" he pledged, "I will not forget thy word." That pledge he kept to the end of his life at age thirty-nine.

**The First Pentecost**

On the day of the first Pentecost, the Holy Spirit descended in power and cut through rivalries and human divisions. Present that day were Parthians, and Medes, and Elamites, and the dwellers in Mesopotamia, and in Judea, and Cappadocia, in Pontus and Asia, Phrygia and Pamhylia, in Egypt and in the parts of Libya about Cyrene and strangers of Rome, Jews, and proselytes, Cretes and Arabians. What an assembly that was! How many differences of customs, of language, of ideologies there were among them. Certainly the likelihood of their coming to a common understanding was as remote as genuine peace appears to be in the Middle East today. But the marvel was that as Peter and the others spoke, all heard the words in their own language. The words that came were not strange. They were clothed in garments that were familiar and yet renewing and revelatory. They came with power, with tongues of fire, and the people could but respond, "Men and brethren, what shall we do?"

As the wind of the Spirit blew and the tongues of flame descended upon them they began their witness that very day. One of the powerful images in this story is that the tongues of flame did not encompass everyone in one big flame. There were individual tongues of flame. One resting on Peter would make a different man from one resting on John. The Spirit is one, but the manifestation of the Spirit differs as it comes in contact with each of us. The work of the Spirit is to allow individual potential to move toward fulfillment, but, as is true in a great orchestra, individual instruments are tuned to be in harmony with every other instrument so great music can be provided.

What images would you use to symbolize the coming of the Holy Spirit to you? Would you use different images for different times? The mystics have said that the coming of the Spirit is "ineffable," inexpressible; and yet everyone of us will try to give expression to this highpoint of human experience. Put down, write down if you wish, an experience of the coming of the Spirit to you. What words or symbols would you use?

**PRAYER:** In symbol of gentle dove and consuming flame, we give image to your Spirit, O God. We have felt its stirrings in he past, and with full expectations await its coming in each new day. We affirm your Spirit upon us, for we are yours. You have captured and claimed us, and we delight in the declaration of your constant workings among humanity. We crown you through Jesus Christ, Lord of all, and join with the Saints of all the ages in singing our alleluia. And may that alleluia be on our lips both now and when we take our final breath of precious life. Amen.

## MONDAY, PENTECOST WEEK
## ORDINARY PEOPLE, EXTRAORDINARY GRACE

**SCRIPTURE:** **Acts 2:17-19 The Work of the Spirit**

*"In the last days it will be, God declares, that I will pour out my Spirit upon all flesh, and your sons and your daughters shall prophesy, and your young men shall see visions and your old men shall dream dreams."*

**Acts 4:13 The Ordinary Becomes Extraordinary**

*When they saw the courage of Peter and John and realized that they were unschooled, ordinary men, they were astonished and they took note that these men had been with Jesus.*

**Acts 4:33 Great Grace Was upon Them**

*With great power the apostles gave their testimony to the resurrection of the Lord Jesus, and great grace was upon them.*

**MEDITATION: A Freeing and Transforming Spirit**

Think of some of the persons present that Pentecost day. Think of the apostles. They were not learned men; at least for the most part they were uneducated: fishermen and other quite ordinary people. They were not teachers or orators. Before now none of them had evidenced a gift for eloquence or persuasive speech; indeed, Peter rarely opened his mouth without putting his foot in it. But now the Spirit has freed and transformed them, and moved them to fluency; they speak without fear or hesitancy, speak in a way that draws people to listen. And those who listen have also been touched and changed by the Spirit. Their ears are opened to hear, each in the way he needs to hear, each in the manner – the language, we might say – that speaks to the heart. When we speak in the Spirit, the Spirit takes our stammering and shapes it into words that express truth. When we are moved by the Spirit to listen, our hearts are opened and we hear with new ears, each in the way that speaks to our particular understanding. In a way, this is the reversal of Babel. What had been scattered now has been unified in Christ through the power of the Spirit. By listing all the nations people have come from, those people who now have become witnesses to the Spirit's coming, Luke indicates that Christ's message will be spread throughout the world and that it will be received and understood everywhere. His redeeming love will be made known in shared witness.

Sermon prepared by Cindy Mortus for Pentecost Sunday, 2005;
Cindy passed away on June 10, 2005

It is no small matter in the history of civilization that ordinary people, men and women, are called to a prophetic vocation, to be bearers of the Spirit. We are the sons and the daughters who shall prophesy. We are the ones who will be part of the wonders in heaven above and signs on the earth below. Do you believe that? If you do, how much are you willing to expend in personal preparation and commitment to be such a prophetic people?

**"In the Last Days It Will Be, God Declares"**

In September 1985, before women were ordained to the priesthood in the Community of Christ (RLDS), I was asked to be the guest minister at a priesthood retreat in Michigan. It was held to help prepare the one hundred male priesthood present for a change in the ministerial service of the church, the coming of women into the priesthood. This was just a few weeks before the first women were ordained and before I had been called to the priesthood. My major assignment was for the Saturday evening session. The class was titled, "Perspectives on Ministry." Realizing the importance of the presentation, I worked hard in preparation and ended up with twenty pages of notes written on my computer. By the time I got to the twentieth page I was weary and just wanted to be done with it. Earlier I had decided to end with Peter's words quoting Joel on the day of Pentecost:

> *In the last days it will be, God declares, that I will pour out my Spirit upon all flesh, and your sons and your daughters shall prophesy, and your young men shall see visions, and your old men shall dream dreams.*

But as I started typing the words, they were no longer words just printed on the computer screen. They came alive. I was flooded with the Spirit and for a few minutes could just sit and weep. What I knew that day was that these words were also spoken to me, that I, too, was called to be a bearer of that Spirit. But more than that, I knew it was a universal call. Everyone who desired could be a bearer of that Spirit if they opened themselves to its influence.

That Saturday evening when I spoke to that group assembled in Sanford, Michigan, the same Spirit that had been with me in preparation descended upon them. The program called for a period of discussion. It didn't happen. For a few moments there was silence and then the men, one by one, some with tears in their eyes, stood and testified about their personal experiences both of struggle and affirmation as the Spirit helped them adjust to this historic moment in the church. The Spirit that we knew that night, though it did not come with flames was the same Spirit present at Pentecost. We, too, under its influence asked, "Brothers, what shall we do?" We knew the days ahead would not be easy but we each had our assignment for furthering the work of the kingdom.

**PRAYER:** Creator God, creating still, By will and work and deed,
Create a new humanity To meet the present need.

Redeemer God, redeeming still, With overflowing grace,
Pour out your love on us, through us; Make this a holy place.

Sustainer God, sustaining still, With strength for every day,
Empower us now to do your will, Recall us when we stray.

Almighty God, for this new day, We need your presence still.
Create, redeem, sustain us now To do your work and will. Amen.

Jane Parker Huber, *Hymns of the Saints,* No. 190

# TUESDAY, PENTECOST WEEK: "REPENT AND BE BAPTIZED"

**SCRIPTURE:** **Acts 2:32-42 All of Us Are Witnesses**

*This Jesus God raised up, and of that all of us are witnesses. Being therefore exalted at the right hand of God, and having received from the Father the promise of the Holy Spirit, he has poured out this that you both see and hear ...Now when they heard this, they were cut to the heart and said to Peter and to the other apostles, "Brothers, what should we do?" Peter said to them, "Repent, and be baptized every one of you in the name of Jesus Christ so that your sins may be forgiven; and you will receive the gift of the Holy Spirit." So those who welcomed his message were baptized, and that day about three thousand persons were added. They devoted themselves t o the apostles' teaching and fellowship, to the breaking of bread and the prayers.*

**MEDITATION: The First Christian Sermon**

Luke records Peter' sermon in considerable detail, and with good reason: it is a masterful piece of gospel proclamation. He first explains the supernatural behavior going on as a fulfillment of Joel's prophecy that the Spirit will be poured out upon all flesh. Next he confronts his hearers with three great facts. Fact 1: God commended Jesus by "*deeds of power, wonders, and signs.*" Fact 2: In spite of this, Jesus was murdered "*by the hands of those outside the law.*" Fact 3: God raised Jesus from the grave, "*having freed him from death, an event that King David himself prophesied.*" Finally, he draws the irrefutable conclusion: "*Therefore, let the entire house of Israel know with certainty that God has made him both Lord and Messiah, this Jesus whom you crucified* (Acts 2:14-36). Pointed, powerful penetrating gospel proclamation.

Well, the Spirit strikes home with Peter's message: the people are "*cut to the heart*" and cry out, "*What should we do?*" Peter is ready with an answer: "*Repent, and be baptized every one of you in the name of Jesus Christ so that your sins may be forgiven*" (Acts 2:38). That day three thousand receive saving grace and immediately move into God's new community. "*They devoted themselves to the apostles' teaching and fellowship, to the breaking of bread and the prayers*" (Acts 2:42). It is hard to improve upon this witness and these results.

Richard J. Foster, *Streams of Living Water,* 200-201; used with permission

**The Word of God Is Sacramental**

The Word of God is sacramental. That means it is sacred, and as a sacred word it makes present what it indicates. When Jesus spoke to the two sad travelers on the road [to Emmaus} and explained to them the words of scripture that were about himself, their hearts began to burn, that is to say, they experienced his presence ...Through his words he became really present to them. That is what we mean by the sacramental quality of the word. The word creates what it expresses. The Word of God is always sacramental ...When we say that God's word is sacred, we mean that God's word is full of God's presence ...The word that is read

> and spoken wants to lead us into God's presence and transform our hearts and minds. Often we think of the word as an exhortation to go out and change our lives. But the full power of the word lies, not in how we apply it to our lives after we have heard it, but in its transforming power that does its divine work as we listen ... The Word of God is not a word to apply to our daily lives at some later date; it is a word to heal us through, and in, our listening here and now
>
> Henri Nouwen, *With Burning Hearts,* 45-47; used with permission.

These words of Henri Nouwen are somewhat frightening to those of us who have the responsibility of representing Christ through the spoken word. We know we are only a vehicle through which the Spirit can work, but though we carry this treasure in earthen vessels, we wish to present ourselves as a worthy vessel for this holy task. We have all known the deeply humbling experience of being used as an instrument for God's presence to move as a healing dove among the people. It is a transforming experience never to be forgotten. But the listener to the word carries equal responsibility. Without some practice and sensitivity to the still, small voice of God, the transforming power can be missed.

Cyril of Jerusalem taught that the spirit is working constantly to enable its witnesses to "speak without deficiency" and its hearers to "hear with discretion." Can you recall times when you have been able to bring the presence of God to the people through "the Word"? Can you also recall when you have been recipients to such presence as a listener to the Word? How do you prepare to be either a bearer or a receiver of the Word?

**PRAYER:** In humility, O God, we recognize that you have called each of us to be your representatives here on earth. You have asked us to be partners with you in your great work of redemption. When we speak for you either in formal or informal situations may we truly be carriers of your word to those who need to hear. But there is so much we ourselves need to hear and learn. In situations where that is possible for us, awaken our minds and spirits to respond and allow your presence to fill us, we pray. Amen.

# WEDNESDAY, PENTECOST WEEK: THE CHURCH IS FORMED

**SCRIPTURE:** **Acts 2:42-43, 46-47** **The Lord Added to Their Number Daily**

They devoted themselves to the apostles' teaching and to the fellowship, to the breaking of bread and to prayer. Everyone was filled with awe, and many wonders and miraculous signs were done by the apostles ...And the Lord added to their number daily those who were being saved.

**MEDITATION: Planting the Seed that Became the Church**

Jesus called, prepared, and empowered not separate individuals, but a group of women and men to be the nucleus of God's renewing grace in and for the world. They stumblingly followed him, endured the devastation of his death, were reclaimed by the miracle of Easter, and sent into all the world in the power of the Spirit. Jesus knew that following him could never be a solo performance; thus he taught the disciples to pray not

"my Father" but "our Father, who are in heaven." He promised them that in the future he always would be present in their midst when they gathered in his name (Matthew 18:20). At his last meal , he told all of the disciples to drink from the cup, not just one or two, and he declared that his death would be for the many, not for the few (Matthew 26:27-28). And after Easter, it was in breaking bread together that his followers found renewed confirmation of his risen presence.

By planting the seed that became the church, Jesus revealed that the renewal of our humanity would not be found apart from life in the company of those who trust in him. The church is not an afterthought to the good news: it is an integral part of the good news ...

> The church is God's unfinished project. Called and empowered by the Spirit, the Christian community is nevertheless made up of fallible and broken people. But thankfully perfection is not a prerequisite for belonging to the church. As Jesus' first disciples often failed to live out his claim on their lives, so the church always stands in need of the grace and forgiveness it proclaims. Like those first disciples, the church is ever on the Way. Living in sacred community is not easy. It involves suffering, struggle and disappointment. God's boundless love meets stiff resistance in human hearts, a fact as true inside the church as outside it. God's work of renewal and reconciliation will never be finished this side of the kingdom. The church must therefore always see itself as a sojourning people; its practices and beliefs will always stand in need of renewal and reform, and its life will be marked by the need for constant repentance.
>
> Anthony Chvala-Smith, *Understanding the Way*, 42, 44

**Koinonia**

In the fifty days between Easter and Pentecost, the disciples were growing up together, helping one another come of age. They met together, prayed together, and waited together. Pentecost, wrote Thomas Keating, is "the feast of spiritual maturity" (*Crisis of Faith, Crisis of Love,* 9). What happened after Pentecost was an intensification of group activity, the *koinonia,* or fellowship that so marked the early Christian church. "How can we comprehend the significance of Pentecost," Marjorie Thompson has asked, "if we do not experience the grace of the Holy Spirit in a living community of faith. How can we understand the mission of the church if we are isolated from the church?" (*Soul Feast,* 56-57).

> Precious as solitude is to each of us, spiritual maturity is possible only through communal support and participation. That is why we do not enter the body of Christ as whole, fulfilled persons. We enter because we are committed and need support for our spiritual journey. Spirituality begins, wrote Urban Holmes, in the human capacity for relationship (*Spirituality for Ministry, 12).* We cannot do it alone. We enter the church because we have said "yes" to Christ's call and wish to become worthy disciples. We experience and find God in relationships. Corporate spirituality is spirituality shared with others. It is the fellowship of a group held together by a passionately shared faith. It is a community of love. It is a community that does not stop with self, but extends its ministry to the whole world.
>
> Velma Ruch, *The Transforming Power of Prayer,* Vol. 2, 108-109

**The Blessed Community**

When we are drowned in the overwhelming seas of the love of God, we find ourselves in a new and particular relation to a few of our fellows. The relation is so surprising and so rich that we despair of finding a word glorious enough and weighty enough to name it. The word *Fellowship* is discovered, but the word is pale and thin in comparison with the rich volume and luminous bulk and warmth of the experience which it would designate. For a new kind of life-sharing and of love has arisen of which we had had only dim hints before. Are these the bonds of love which knit together the early Christians, the very warp and woof of the Kingdom of God? In glad amazement and wonder we enter upon a relationship which we had not known the world contained for the sons of men. Why should such bounty be given to unworthy persons like ourselves?...

"See how these Christians love one another" might well have been a spontaneous exclamation in the days of the apostles. The Holy Fellowship, the Blessed Community has always astonished those who stood without it. The sharing of physical goods in the primitive church is only an outcropping of a profoundly deeper sharing of a Life, the base and center of which is obscured, to those who are still oriented about self, rather than about God. To others, tragic to say, the very existence of such a Fellowship within a common Life and Love is unknown and unguessed. In its place, psychological and humanistic views of the essential sociality and gregariousness of man seek to provide a social theory of church membership. From these views spring church programs of mere sociability and social contacts. The precious word *Fellowship* becomes identified with a purely horizontal relation of man to man, not with that horizontal-vertical relationship of man to man *in God.*

> But every period of profound re-discovery of God's joyous immediacy is a period of emergence of this amazing group inter-knittedness of God-enthralled men and women who know one another *in Him* ...It is the holy matrix of "the communion of the saints," the body of Christ, which is His church.
>
> Thomas R. Kelly, *A Testament of Devotion,* 77, 79-80; used with permission

**PRAYER:**

Beloved community of God, In vision seen, a perfect whole
All that we have we pledge to thee, Our powers of body, mind, and soul.

The healthy frame, the steady nerve, The active pulse of flesh and blood,
With these we dedicate to thee Our manhood and our womanhood.

All gains of skill and fruits of thought, Whate'er we know, whate'er we feel,
Humbly we bring that we may prove, True servants of the common weal.

Fair visions of the good and true Wrought into speech and kindly deed,
These be our sacrament of love, Our witness to the Christly creed.

King of the kingdom of our dreams, From dreams we turn to take our part
In that beloved community Where love is law in every heart.
Ernest Dodgshun, *Hymns of the Saints*, No. 414

# THURSDAY, PENTECOST WEEK: GOD'S VOICE CONTINUES TO BE HEARD

**SCRIPTURE:** **John 16:12-13 Getting Ready to Hear.**

"*I still have many things to say to you but you cannot bear them now.*"

**Doctrine and Covenants, 162:2a Let the Spirit Breathe**

*Again you are reminded that this community was divinely called into being. The spirit of the Restoration is not locked in one moment of time, but is instead the call to every generation to witness to essential truths in its own language and form. Let the Spirit breathe.*

**MEDITATION: Pentecost in Our Day**

On April 6, 1830, a group of six men met in Fayette, New York, and organized the church first known simply as the Church of Christ but with the belief that they were called to be part of the building of Zion, the kingdom of God on earth. How could that pitifully small group proclaim that they were called to such a work? No doubt because they, too, felt the anointing of which Jesus spoke when he said, "*The Spirit of the Lord is upon me for he has anointed me to bring good news.*" They believed, as do we, that if they kept the commandments and sought to bring forth and establish the cause of Zion the mysteries of God would be unfolded to them. Thy believed if they asked they would receive revelation upon revelation, knowledge upon knowledge, that they might know the mysteries and peaceable things that bring joy and life eternal. Sometimes they, we, really did mess things up but like Christ's acceptance of Peter, God does not give up easily. Through the Spirit we are lifted up again and again and asked to try once more. This is such a time.

**A Called-Out People**

At various times in history God has called out a people with the potential, under prophetic leadership, to be in the forefront of Christ's body on earth. The Restoration people of God are such a people. We are only beginning to understand and fulfill our calling in this regard.

In 1950 Israel A. Smith wrote,

> *The voice of inspiration directs me to say: The church as a whole is commended for the spiritual growth and the preparation of the priesthood... This necessary work should proceed...in preparation for the greater endowment of spiritual power which has been promised and which awaits the time when they can receive it*
>
> (D. and C. 142:4).

Although God is at work among all people, the Creator has called out individuals and groups of people, formed under prophetic leadership, for special roles in bringing forth Zionic living on earth. A Restoration people and the Temple in the Center Place are part of that process.

The Book of Acts tells of spiritual endowment, enlarging dimensions of ministry, new understandings, and expanding beliefs which were challenging and joyous to many, but not to all. We also are individually and collectively as a people facing new frontiers. The

Lord who is leading us on has yet many things to say to us ...While Joseph Smith, Jr., was praying for direction, he experienced a vision and heard a voice saying of Jesus, "*This is my beloved Son, hear him*!" Thus was established the roots of the Restoration movement. This new thrust of God into history was inseparably a part of the ongoing purposes of the Lord in the course of time. It was a call away from creedal Christianity. Restoration identity is not a package of doctrinal beliefs or a form of church organization. The Restoration established a people under prophetic leadership to continue the spiritual journey that moves toward the accomplishment of Zionic life on earth.

John Conway, "Restoration Identity – The Faith Journey of a People," in Temple School course TL 103 Abundant Life and the Temple, 77-78

We limit not the truth of God To our poor reach of mind
By notions of our day and sect, Crude, partial, and confined.
No, let a new and better hope Within our hearts be stirred –
The Lord hath yet more light and truth To break forth from his word.

Who dares to bind to their dull sense The oracles of heaven
For all the nations, tongues, and climes, And all the ages given?
That universe, how much unknown! That ocean unexplored!
The Lord hath yet more light and truth To break forth from his word.

O Father, Son and Spirit, send Us increase from above;
Enlarge, expand all Christian souls To comprehend thy love,
And make us all go on to know, With nobler powers conferred,
The Lord hath yet more light and truth To break forth from his word.

George Rawson, *Hymns of the Saints,* No. 309

**PRAYER:**

Master, speak! Thy servant heareth! Make me wise that I may see
What I need that I may follow With a step more firm and free.

Through the ages thou hast spoken To the seers who called on thee,
So in prayer I claim thy promise, Master, speak! O speak to me!

Speak, O Christ, and through the stillness whisper "I have chosen you/"
Tell me in this high communion What it is that I should do.

Master, speak! Thy servant heareth! And where'er thy voice is heard
Let me comprehend thy message And reveal in life thy word.

Roy A. Cheville, *Hymns of the Saints,* No. 410

# FRIDAY, PENTECOST WEEK: COMMUNITY RESPONSE TO THE WORD

**SCRIPTURE:** **Doctrine and Covenants 161:3c Vibrant Witnesses**

*Be patient with one another, for creating sacred community is arduous and even painful. But it is to loving community such as that each is called. Be courageous and visionary, believing in the power of just a few vibrant witnesses to transform the world. Be assured that love will overcome the voices of fear, division, and deceit.*

**Doctrine and Covenants 161:6 a,b A Global Family United in Christ**

Stand firm in the name of the One you proclaim and create diverse communities of disciples and seekers, rejoicing in the continuing fulfillment of the call to this people to prophetically witness in the name of Jesus Christ.

Heed the urgent call to become a global family united in the name of the Christ, committed in love to one another, seeking the kingdom for which you yearn and to which you have always been summoned. That kingdom shall be a peaceable one and it shall be known as Zion.

**MEDITATION: Redemptive Ministries**

We are called to be partners of a God of blessing, to be ministers to a world in need of healing and salvation. It is an awesome and humbling task that calls for total commitment on our part and daily growth in the Spirit. That is what spiritual formation is all about. The road we are asked to travel can be a road of miracle as ordinary men and women and children rise above themselves, get attached to the eternal reservoir of God's grace and truth and power and become themselves transmitters of the light of the Divine. In the process we gain spiritual authority. When the question comes to as – and it will sometime and someplace – our answer will involve more than the acceptance of the commission "Go tell!" It will require that we become the embodiment of what we speak. It will require us to express a love we cannot know and a light we cannot reveal unless we have first received it in association with the Christ.

The endowment of the Spirit for which we wait is an endowment for redemptive ministries. As Mary Sue Gast has written,

> Even now the flames may dance above our heads.
> Igniting our opinions on peacemaking so that they blaze into commitment.
> Even now the flames may be burning into our hearts. Animating us,
> leaving us no peace as individuals until God's justice and peace fill the
> earth as the waters fill the seas.
>
> In Ruth C. Duck and Maren C. Tirabassi, eds., *Touch Holiness*
> (New York: The Pilgrim Press, 1993), 93

We, too, can be touched by holy fire. Our problem in such a dream is not that we hope for too much but that we hope for too little. God is waiting to pour out blessings on us as we become willing to receive. Then we will exclaim with the early Christians, "*How immense are the resources of his grace, and how great his kindness to us in Christ Jesus*" (Ephesians 2:7 NEB).

> Created in God's image and called to grow in God's likeness, as transformed beings through the power of the Spirit, we will devote ourselves to the mission of Christ Jesus as we work for the blessing and salvation of humankind. That is our call. That is our task. We will not forget. Amen.
>
> Velma Ruch, *The Transforming Power of Prayer,* Vol. 2, 193-194

As Christians and as members and friends of the Community of Christ we are indeed living in a time of very special demands. We are called to a new creation, to spiritual awakening, to a ministry of peace, reconciliation, and healing of the spirit. This call is not ours alone, designed for our personal salvation, but it is one in which all the world's people can share. The great adventure to which we are called will mean new life styles, new ways of understanding, a difference in our work, in economics, in politics, in government. Most of all it will depend upon our ability to remain whole and radiant, carrying the presence of the Divine into every situation in which we find ourselves. Abraham was once called upon to walk into a new land, a land to which God called him. He went, perhaps not without some fear and trepidation, but he went and he was blessed. Let us not be afraid to walk into our new land, a land into which God is leading us and there make the contribution which is ours to make. What is your answer?

PRAYER: Holy Spirit of God, who gathers the church into one body, gather us once again in your presence and strengthen the bonds of affection that hold your people together. Bless us with grace to cooperate with one another in love and service that we may be the signs of your uniting love to our fractured world. Teach us to show compassion for those in need, to face challenges with imagination, and to counter disappointments with prayerful trust. So may your church bring forth your will and your reign. Amen.

Duck and Tirabassi, *Touch Holiness*

# SATURDAY, PENTECOST WEEK: BOLDLY ENVISION THE FUTURE

**SCRIPTURE:** **Doctrine and Covenants 161:1 a,b The Place Beyond the Horizon**

Lift up your eyes and fix them on the place beyond the horizon to which you are sent. Journey in trust, assured that the great and marvelous work is for this time and for all time. Claim your unique and sacred place within the circle of those who call upon the name of Jesus Christ. Be faithful to the spirit of the Restoration, mindful that it is a spirit of adventure, openness, and searching. Walk proudly and with a quickened step. Be a joyful people. Laugh and play and sing, embodying the hope and freedom of the gospel.

**Doctrine and Covenants 162:8 c. Continue Your Journey**

*Continue your journey, O people of the Restoration. You have been blessed thus far but there is so much yet to see, so much yet to do. Go forth with confidence and live prophetically as a people who have been loved, and who now courageously choose to love others in the name of the One you serve. Amen.*

**MEDITATION: Draw Near to God**

We have the promise, "*Draw near to God, and he will draw near to you*" (James 4:8). But that drawing near is costly. For most of us the earlier and easier days of our discipleship are behind us. We are called to mount a higher rung in the service of our Lord. Such spiritual maturity and the service it calls forth has a price. We become aware of our own failings and stubborn resistance to being immersed in the refining fire. We recognize some of the cost of bearing one another's burdens. We realize that our lives are not ours to spend as we choose. This is so whether we find ourselves in the valley or in the perceived sunshine of divine presence.

Daily we discover that we have undertaken a journey that does not proceed on level ground. The landscape is filled with mountains and valleys, neither one of which could exist without the other, as the concept of light could not be if it were not for darkness. We often discover we are called to walk where the rocks are rough and our feet are rubbed raw, where we may slip and slide, but we continue because we know that God's loving Spirit has not deserted us. Out of the rocks and the seemingly barren landscape, a dove returns with a slip of an olive branch in its beak and we are confronted with a promise of a new world yet to be. With renewed courage we continue our journey.

**A New World in the Making**

The great experience of the Word that became flesh, the Incarnation, must be reexperienced and reexpressed in every individual and find its apotheosis in corporate form, the kingdom of God among us. The desire to do so is as old as humanity itself. It was the ancient dream of a Golden Age; it was the hope for a New Jerusalem; it was Utopia; it was Zion.

Never, perhaps, has the world more desperately needed those who can develop a spiritual power that matches and is effectively coordinated with intellectual competence. We cannot pretend that the past two centuries of the development of knowledge is of no concern to us or that the church has no use for the questions and discoveries of the analytic mind. Our challenge is to inject into the glories of this intelligence a vision of the kingdom of God that can fulfill what we know by what we become. Unfortunately, even in the church of Christ we have a scarcity of those whose intellectual competence is shot through with the radiance of the Spirit of God. A partial result of this is a separation of the private and public realms of our lives. Admittedly, it is difficult in our current society to proclaim in the workplace our religious commitment, but it is possible to become contagious persons whose inward spirit will communicate beyond words. It is Presence that makes the difference.

That "beloved community of God," which is the joyful community of Saints, is more than a dream. Wherever there is a saintly person – wherever there is a group, however small, whose members enact the purpose of their creation – there, the places which they occupy do indeed shine as Zion, the redeemed of the Lord. We need not know their names – many will remain nameless and will not receive worldly fame – but their influence will be potent through the generations. They will be for us the signature of God. Is it possible that we, too, could be one of them? These scriptures and meditation in which we have engaged are designed for exactly that purpose.

To what are you willing to commit yourself?

PRAYER: Lord Jesus, of you I will sing as I journey.
I'll tell all my neighbours about you wherever I go
You alone give us life, give us peace, give us love.
Lord Jesus, of you I will sing as I journey.

Lord Jesus, I'll praise you as long as I journey.
May all of my joy be a faithful reflection of you.
May the earth and the sea and the sky join my song.
Lord Jesus, I'll praise you as long as I journey.

As long as I live, Jesus, make me your servant,
to carry your cross and to share all your burdens and tears;
for you save us by giving your body and blood.
As long as I live, Jesus, make me your servant.

I fear in the dark and the doubt of my journey,
but courage will come with the sound of your steps by my side.
And with all of the people you saved by your love,
we'll sing to the dawn at the end of our journey.

Les Petites Soeurs de Jesus, rev. Eng. Stephen Somerville,
*Sing for Peace*, No. 31

# WORKS CITED

(The page number following each citation refers to the page number in which the quotation appears in this book.)

Augustine, *The Confessions of Saint Augustine,* John K Ryan, trans. (New York: Image Doubleday, 1960), 28, 68, 70.

Barkley, William. *The Gospel of John* (Philadelphia: The Westminster Press, 1975), 25.
*The Acts of the Apostles* (Westminster: John Knox Press, 1976), 101-102.

Ben Judah, Daniel. "Praise to the Living God," *Hymns of the Saints,* No. 47, 55.

Bergan, Jacqueline Syrup and S. Marie Schwan. *Freedom: A Guide for Prayer* (Winona, Minnesota: Saint Mary's Press, 1988), 8, 24, 29.
*Surrender: A Guide for Prayer* (Winona, Minnesota: St. Mary's Press, 1986), 26.

Bernard of Clairvaux, *On the Song of Songs* (London: Mowbray and Co.,1952}, 42.
"Jesus, the Very Thought of Thee," *Hymns of the Saints,* No. 282, 42.

*Bhagavad-Gita: The Song of God,* Swami Prabhanvananda and Christopher Isherwood, trans. (New York: Mentor Religious Classics, 1951), 53-54.

Bonar, Horatio, "O Love of God, How Strong and True," *Hymns of the Saints,* No. 188, 53.

Bode, John E. "O, Jesus, I Have Promised," *Hymns of the Saints,* No. 463, 94.

Booth, Paul. "Spiritual Awakening." Sermon Given at 1986 World Conference, 104.

Broome, J. H. *Pascal* (New York: Barnes and Noble, 1965), 122.

Brother Lawrence. *Practicing the Presence,* Gene Edwards, ed. (Auburn, Maine:Christian Books, 1976), 78.

Buechner, Fredrick. *The Hungering Dark* (HarperSanFrancisco, 1969), 87.

Capote, Truman. *A Christmas Memory.* Quoted in *Alive Now* (November/December, 1994), 22.

Chvala-Smith, Anthony. *Understanding the Way* (Herald House, 2003), 22-23, 128.

Cheville, Roy. "Master Speak, Thy Servant Heareth," *Hymns of the Saints,* No. 410, 132.
"Open My Eyes, O Lord," *Hymns of the* Saints, No. 454, 45.

Chittister, Joan. "Yesterday's Dangerous Vision," *Sojourners* (July 1987), 88-89.

Conway, John. "Restoration Identity – The Faith Journey of a People" in Temple School course TL 103 Abundant Life and the Temple, 132.

Coffman, Linda. "He Lives in Us," *Hymns of the Saints,* No.199, 98.

Custer, Chester E. "O Christ, My Lord, Create in Me," *Hymns of the Saints,* No.174, 105.

Dearman, Kirk and Deby. "Lord, Make Us Instruments of Your Peace," *Sing a New Song,* No. 21, 120.

Dodgshun, Ernest. "Beloved Community of God," *Hymns of the Saints,* No. 414, 130.

Doughty, Stephen V. "How Do We Pray If We Are Divided?" *Weavings* (July/August 2000), 73.

Douglas, Deborah Smith, "Vine and Branches: Abiding in Christ," *Weavings* (September/October 2001), 67.

"Do You Want to Be Healed?" *Weavings* (September/October 1995), 81-82.

Edwards, Tilden. "Living the Day from the Heart," *The Weavings Reader: Living with God in the World,* John S. Mogabgab, ed. (Nashville: The Upper Room, 1993), 3.

Eliot, T. S. "What the Thunder Said," *The Waste Land* (1922), 10.

Foster, Richard J. "The Incarnational Tradition," *Streams of Living Water* (HarperSanFrancisco, 1998), 21-22, 106.

"The Evangelical Tradition," in *Streams of Living Water,* 126.

*Celebration of Discipline* (San Francisco: Harper and Row, 1978), 46, 74.

In James Bryan Smith, *Embracing the Love of God* (HarperSanFrancisco, 1995), 27-28.

Gallaher, Edith. Sermon preached in Lamoni, Iowa (August 6, 2000), 56-57.

Gire, Ken. "An Intimate Moment with Peter" in *Intimate Moments with the Savior* (Grand Rapids, Michigan: Zondervan, House, 1989), 94-96.

Guenther, Margaret. *Toward Holy Ground* (Boston: Couley Publications, 1995), 111.

Hamarskjold, Dag. *Markings,* Leif Sjoberg and W. H. Auden, trans. (New York: Alfred A Knopf, 1964), 69.

Havergal, Francis Ridley. "I Am Trusting Thee, Lord Jesus," *Hymns of the Saints,* No. 127, 73.

Hedge, Frederick Henry. "Sovereign and Transforming Grace," *Hymns of the Saints,* No. 12, 58.

Higdon, Barbara. "A Time of True Shalom," in *Shepherds Abiding in the Field,* Leonard Young, ed. (Herald House, 1997), 106-109.

Holliday, Tacy. "Waiting," Meditation for Pentecost, 100.

Hopkins, Gerard Manley. "The Wreck of the Deutschland," Pt. 1, line 40, 36.

Huber, Jane Parker. "Creator God, Creating Still," *Hymns of the* Saints, No. 190, 125.

Hunker, E. Y. "When Kindled by the Spirit's Light," *Hymns of the Saints,* No.282, 42.

James, Ron. *A Joy Wider than the World* (Nashville: Upper Room Books, 1992), 80.

Job, Rueben P. *A Guide to Prayer for All Who Seek God* (Nashville: Upper Room Books, 2003), 99.

Johnson, Ben Campbell. *Discerning God's Will* (Louisville: Westminster/John Knox Press, 1990), 46.

*Living Before God* (Grand Rapids, Michigan: Wm. B. Eerdmans, 2000), 51.

Jones, W. Paul. "Joy and Religious Motivation," *Weavings* (November/December 1995), 119.

Keating, Thomas. *Crisis of Faith, Crisis of Love* (New York: Continuum Publishing Company, 1995), 7.

Kelley, Thomas. *A Testament of Devotion,* Biographical Memoir by Douglas V. Steere (New York: Harper and Row, 1941), 51, 58, 63, 78, 129.

Kierkegaard, Soren. Quoted in Jaques Colette, ed. *Kierkegaard: The Difficulty of Being Christian* (The University of Notre Dame Press, 1960), 116.

Killinger, John. *Christ in the Seasons of Ministry* (Waco, Texas: Word Books, 1983), 18, 20, 93.

Larcom, Lucy. "Draw Thou My Soul, O Christ," *Hymns of the Saints*, No.168, 79.

Lathbury, Mary A. "Break Thou the Bread of Life," *Hymns of the Saints,* No.173, 56.

Lucado, Max. *No Wonder They Call Him Savior* (Portland, Oregon: Multnomah Press, 1986), 120.

Miller, Wendy J. *Jesus Our Spiritual Director* (Nashville: Upper Room Books, 2004), 19.

Milton, John. "Areopagitica," *Complete Poems and Major Prose,* ed. Merritt Y. Hughes (New York:Odyssey Press, 1957), 31.

"Samson Agonistes," 33.

"On Christian Doctrine," 54.

Mogabgab, John. "Editor's Introduction," *Weavings* (September/October 2001), 66.

Moon, Cleo Hanthorne, "Help Us Express Your Love, O Lord," *Hymns of the Saints,* No. 415, 84

"Here We Have Come, Dear Lord, To Thee," *Hymns of the Saints*, No.109, 110.

"The Weight of Past and Fruitless Guilt," *Hymns of the* Saints, No. 118, 92.

Mortus, Cindy. Sermon prepared for Pentecost (Hampton, Virginia, 2005), 97, 124.

Murphy, Scott. Letter to Lamoni Heartland Mission, 106.

Newton, John. "Amazing Grace," *Hymns of the Saints,* No. 104, 71.

Nouwen, Henri J. M. *With Burning Hearts: A Meditation on the Eucharistic Life* (Maryknoll, New York: Orbis Books, 1994), 10-11, 12-13, 15, 127.

Oden, Thomas. *The Transforming Power of Grace* (Nashville: Abdingdon Press, 1993), 71, 72.

Palmer, Roy. "My Faith Looks Up to Thee," *Hymns of the Saints,* No.143, 113.

Peck, Scott. *The Road Less Traveled* (Simon and Schuster, 1978), 72-73.

Plaskett, Douglas. *Pulpit Digest* (July/August 1982), 68-69.

Prevallet, Elaine M. "Finding the Way," *Weavings* (November/December 2001), 64-65.
Price, Phyllis. "Prayer of the Storyteller," *Holy Fire* (Mahwah, New Jersey: Paulist Press, 1998), 115-16.
"Homeless," ibid., 70.

Rawson, George. "We Limit Not the Truth of God," *Hymns of the Saints,* No. 309, 132.

*Renovare Spiritual Formation Bible.* Richard J. Foster, ed. (HarperSanFrancisco, 2005), 11, 12, 53, 54-55, 93.

Ruch, Velma. *The Signature of God* (Herald House, 1986), 36-37, 41-42, 54, 90-91, 104-105.
"The Cross Life: The Spirituality of the Wounded Healer," *Summoned to Pilgrimage* (Herald House, 1994), 32-33.
*The Transforming Power of Prayer,* Vol. 1. (Herald House, 1999) 30, 73, 81.
*The Transforming Power of Prayer,* Vol. 2. (Herald House, 1999), 51-52, 101, 120, 129.
"Sensing the Leading of My Spirit," The Aaronic Priesthood Temple Event (June 30, 1995), 50.
"The Church of Burning Hearts" (unpublished), 38-39.
"The Discipline of Witnessing," *The Order of Evangelists' Training Resource* (1995), 120.

Rupp, Ann Neufeld. "Holy Spirit, Come With Power," *Hymns of the Saints,* No. 287, 44.

Rupp, Joyce. *Fresh Bread* (Notre Dame, Indiana: Ave Maria Press, 1985), 57.

Saint Bernard of Clairvaux. *On the Song of Songs* (London: A. R. Mowbray and Co., 1952), 42.
"Jesus, the Very Thought of Thee," *Hymns of the Saints,* No. 167, 42.

Selden, Eric L. "Lord, Lead Me By Your Spirit," *Hymns of the Saints,* No.183, 59.

Schaal, David. "My Peace I Give You," *Herald* (January 2005), 1.

Smith, James Bryan. *Embracing the Love of God.* Foreword by Richard Foster (HarperSanFrancisco, 1995). 27-28.

Smith, Wallace B. "Wholeness–A Quality of Life-Style," *Saints Herald* (January 1997), 6, 112.

Spencer, Geoffrey. "Now Let Our Hearts Within Us Burn," *Hymns of the Saints,* No. 495, 13.

Steere, Douglas in Thomas Kelley, *A Testament of Devotion* (New York: Harper and Row, 1941), 51.

Stewart, James. *A Man in Christ* (Hodden and Stoughton), 67.

Tagore, Rabindranath. "You Came Down from Your Throne," *Gitanjali* (Boston: International Pocket Library), 86.
"When Thou Commandest Me To Sing," ibid., 87.

Thurman, Howard. "Reconciliation," *Disciplines of the Spirit* (Richmond, Indiana: Friends United Press, 1987, c. 1963), 108-109.

Tillich, Paul. "Spiritual Presence." Sermon preached in Rockefeller Chapel (Chicago, Sunday, January 15, 1961), 43.

*Touch Holiness.* Ruth C. Duck and Maren C. Tirrabassi, eds. (New York: The Pilgrim Press, 1990), 133, 134.

Tzeng, Mickael. "A Daily Prayer for Peace" (Taiwan, September 7, 1999), 107.

Underhill, Evelyn. "Breathing the Air of Eternity," *Weavings* (May/June 2002), 75.

Vaughn, Vicky. "Come, Holy Spirit, Come," *Sing a New Song,* No.6, 36.

Veazey, Stephen M. "Share the Peace of Jesus Christ," *Herald* (July 2005), 8-9.

Walter, Howard Arnold. "I Would Be True," *Hymns of the Saints,* No.404, 89.

Willard, Dallas. *The Spirit of the Disciplines* (HarperSanFrancisco, 1991), 50.

Wright, Wendy M. *The Rising* (Nashville:Upper Room Books, 1994), 2, 62-63, 98.